# The finance and accounting desktop guide

## *Accounting literacy for the non-financial manager*

Ralph Tiffin

THOROGOOD

Thorogood Publishing Ltd
10-12 Rivington Street
London EC2A 3DU

Telephone: 020 7749 4748
Fax: 020 7729 6110
Email: info@thorogoodpublishing.co.uk
Web: www.thorogoodpublishing.co.uk



A CIP catalogue record for this book is available from the British Library.

PB ISBN: 1 85418 309 5
978-185418309-5

RB ISBN: 1 85418 304 4
978-185418304-0

Printed in India by Replika Press

Designed and typeset in the UK by Driftdesign

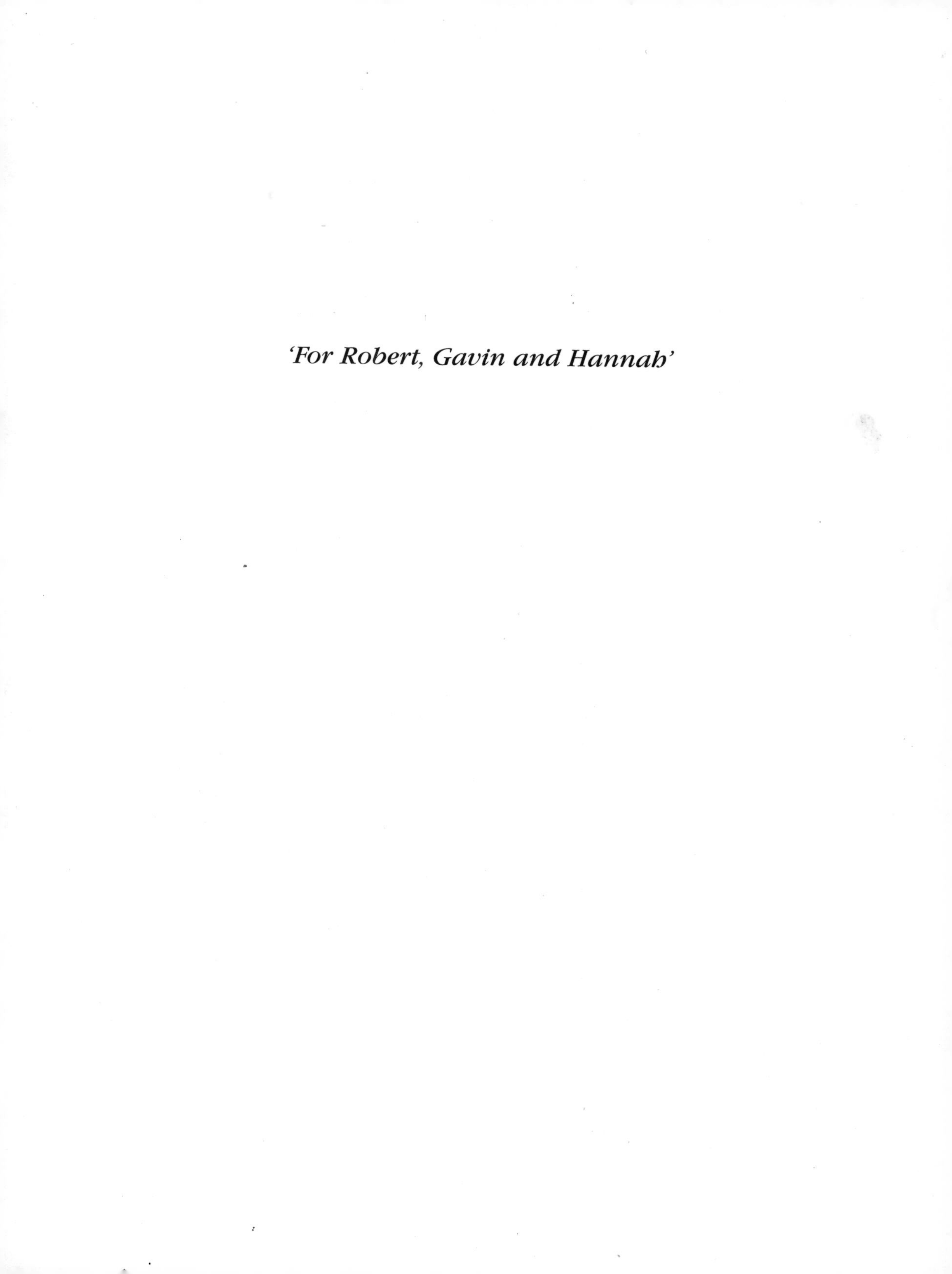

*'For Robert, Gavin and Hannah'*

# CONTENTS

## Icons

Throughout the Desktop Guide series of books you will see references and symbols in the margins. These are designed for ease of use and quick reference directing you to key features of the text. The symbols used are:

definition

question and answer

for example

checklist

# Introduction

## Content and structure

The aim of this text is to explain the meaning and use of the principal accountancy statements, models and activities in business life.

The word 'statements' includes balance sheets, profit and loss accounts, cash flow statements and budget reports.

The word 'models' is used to mean the exercises of costing, cash flow forecasting, capital expenditure appraising and other modelling which is essential for sound business decision making.

The word 'activities' covers the topics of accounting systems and controls, record keeping (book keeping) and the operation of the budget process.

In summary all relevant aspects of business accounting are covered.

## Difficulties in studying accounting

Record keeping, financial reporting and management accounting models are without exception simple in essence. There are areas which may become complicated - often this is due to the amount of detail or the real or perceived need for detailed analysis or disclosure. *For this reason the chapters are split into two sections. This first section explains the basic statements, definitions and models, and the second section explains the topics in more detail and develops the subject as appropriate*.

This approach has been taken to assist the reader to gain a general understanding of business accounting - by reading the first sections and studying the second sections as required. A clear understanding of the principles outlined in the first sections should greatly assist the reader in not being overwhelmed by the volume of detail, variations of essentially simple models and tangential issues which are met in many accounting texts.

## Structure and content detail

The logic of the chapters is to commence with the fundamental financial statements, showing how they are compiled and the need for accounting systems and controls. There is a need for accounting rules and the fundamental financial statements - balance sheets, profit and loss accounts and cash flow statements ........ **1 to 3**

The need for underlying records and accounting systems ........ **4**

Fundamental accounting concepts, the need for rules and accounting standards and detailed accounting policies ........ **5**

How to interpret financial statements ........ **6**

Cash flow forecasting and appraising capital expenditure ........ **7**

Costing in detail and for planning purposes ........ **8 and 9**

Budgeting - the process and how to budget ........ **10**

A study of the first sections in the order outlined should give the reader a clear insight into the main areas of everyday business accounting. There are many examples of statement layouts and where appropriate there are review questions with feedback. The second sections should be consulted where a deeper knowledge of that particular topic is required.

# chapter one

section one

## Balance sheets

## What is a balance sheet?

A balance sheet is a statement compiled at a specific point in time, normally at year, period or month ends. It has two parts or sides which total to exactly equal amounts – it balances! There are many uses of a balance sheet. It could be a control statement – the traditional listing of assets to check that they equal liabilities, or it could be a statement of historical or updated worth of a business. For these and also cultural reasons there are many possible formats for a balance sheet. Contemporary layouts for major trading countries are given in Section 2 of this chapter.

### A simple balance sheet

A simple and useful starting point towards understanding the key totals and sub totals found in balance sheets is to consider what the balance sheets *two sides* contain.

- **Net assets employed**, tangible, intangible and financial assets (buildings, equipment, stock, debtors, cash) less liabilities due to be settled within a short period (a year or much less).

This is the net worth of the business or capital employed in the business as visibly seen, recorded, measured and managed by the directors and employees.

- **What finances the business**, the capital employed in the business, but from the perspective of the investor. It is the owners' and lenders' investment in the business. This side should be exactly equal in amount to the net assets employed side.

**Balance sheet**
***as at (a date)***

| | |
|---|---|
| **Net assets** | X |
| Tangible, physical, measurable assets<br>less short-term liabilities | |
| = | |
| **Finance** | X |
| Share capital plus profits left<br>in the business by the investors plus loans from lenders | |

In accounting terms a balance sheet is a statement of assets and liabilities of a business at a point in time. Assets owe value to the business and liabilities are value owed to others – either third parties (suppliers, tax authorities) or suppliers of finance (shareholders and long-term lenders).

A balance sheet thus shows assets owned and having value less liabilities to third parties – the net worth or net book amount in one section. This is then balanced by an equal amount which represents the amounts owed to the suppliers of the finance – the shareholders and long-term lenders.

**Assets employed**

Fixed assets

\+ Current assets

\- Current liabilities

= **Net worth, net book amount or capital employed**

**Financed by**

Shareholders' Funds or Equity

\+ Long-term finance

= **Total funding, net worth or capital employed**

The balance sheet of a simple business follows the basic definitions below.

## Definition of terms

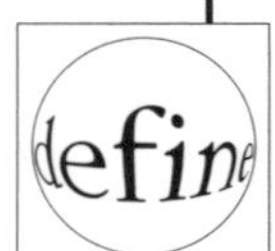


### *Fixed assets*

Normally assets owned by a business and used to produce products and supply services over a number of years. They are most often tangible, physical assets – the infrastructure of a business. They are also assets held for long-term use and are normally not traded on a regular basis.

In simple terms an asset may be defined as fixed if it will be used in more than one accounting period (12 months).

### *Current assets*

Normally assets held or owned by a business which are related to the supply of goods or services – stocks of products, debtors arising from the sale of stocks or supply of services. They are normally assets associated with day to day trading and the aim is to hold them for as short a period as is possible.

In simple terms an asset may be defined as current if its form is expected to change within an accounting period (12 months).

### *Current liabilities*

(Or more formally creditors: amounts falling due within one year.) Normally liabilities associated with day to day trading – overdraft used to finance debtors or purchase stock; creditors for stock purchases employee taxes due on wages/salaries. They are often closely related to current assets, for example trade creditors will be in respect of stock held as current asset. Overdraft may exist to finance stocks or debtors.

A liability must be defined as current if it falls due within 12 months of the balance sheet date.

### *Net current assets (or liabilities)*

This figure is simply the net of current assets minus current liabilities. It is more commonly called working capital.

### *Long-term liabilities*

(Or more formally creditors: amounts falling due after more than one year). Liabilities associated with financing of the business – normally to finance the long-term assets – the fixed assets of a business.

A liability must be defined as long-term if it falls due after more than 12 months from the balance sheet date.

### *Shareholders' funds or equity*

A heading covering the investment by shareholders or equity investors in the business.

*The principal amounts are defined as:*

### *Called up share capital*

The investment made by the shareholders, normally paid to the company in exchange for ordinary shares of a fixed value eg £1 50p or 20p ordinary shares.

### *Profit and loss account*

Profits made in the current and previous periods which have been left in the business and reinvested, rather than withdrawn as dividends. This is also called retained profit or reserves.

eg

**Simple Business**

*Balance sheet as at 31 March 2xx6*

| | | | |
|---|---|---|---|
| **Fixed assets** | Land and Buildings | | 50,100 |
| | Fixtures and Fittings | | 17,800 |
| | Motor Vehicle | | 6,900 |
| | | | **74,800** |
| **Current assets** | Stock | 22,500 | |
| | Debtors | 31,600 | |
| | Cash | 2,200 | |
| | | 56,300 | |
| **Current liabilities** | Overdraft | 13,900 | |
| | Trade Creditors | 23,600 | |
| | Taxation | 8,700 | |
| | | 46,200 | |
| **Net current assets working capital** | | | **10,100** |
| **Net book amount, capital employed or net worth** | | | **84,900** |
| **Financed by:** | | | |
| **Long-term loan** | | | 15,000 |
| **Shareholders' funds** | | | |
| | Share Capital | 20,000 | |
| | Retained Profit and Loss | 49,900 | |
| | | | **69,900** |
| | | | **84,900** |

## What do balance sheets reveal?

g

The first point to remember when interpreting any financial statements is that the figures are not the creation of an accountant, but are meant to faithfully represent the business to which they relate. Careless record keeping (book keeping) inappropriate and inconsistent rules (accounting policies) or deliberate miss statement (fraud!) may of course give unreliable statements, but it is assumed that the reader is dealing with reliable statements.

The following illustration is an example of what is meant by the above assertion:

The balance sheets below, with assets and liabilities expressed as percentages of capital employed are of three different types of business.

X - a general manufacturer

Y - a telecoms utility

Z - a professional practice which leases its office.

| | X | Y | Z |
|---|---|---|---|
| Fixed Assets | 46% | 117% | 15% |
| **current assets** | | | |
| Stock/Work in progress | 64% | 1% | 46% |
| Debtors | 68% | 25% | 62% |
| Cash | 0% | 19% | 0% |
| **current liabilities** | | | |
| Overdraft | -5% | -3% | -15% |
| Creditors | -73% | -59% | -8% |
| | **100%** | **100%** | **100%** |
| | | | |
| Shareholders' Funds | 64% | 40% | 88% |
| Long Term Loans | 36% | 60% | 12% |
| | **100%** | **100%** | **100%** |

**X** has significant percentages of fixed assets – plant and machinery, significant stock/work in progress and debtors matched by significant creditors. What you might expect to find in a general manufacturer's business.

**Y** has a very high percentage of fixed assets and significant debtors. This is what might be expected of a telecoms company with its heavy investment in infrastructure and its customers' credit accounts. The high percentage of long-term loans would also be common in utility companies.

**Z** has significant percentages of work in progress and debtors. These are figures which would be the major assets in a professional firm which does not own its office.

Hopefully the above matching appears reasonable to the reader. It is obviously easy to do this exercise with knowledge of the answer! The point with interpretation of figures is that information should be used firstly to identify key figures. For example, with the utility, the one asset type which it will have above all others is fixed assets. Once key figures are understood and matched, the remainder should fall in place.

There is a review question and feedback which may be used to enhance your interpretation skills and develop an understanding of balance sheet structure. Also in the second section interpretation of balance sheets is covered in much more detail.

## Interpreting balance sheet profiles

Set out below are the principal activities of six companies followed by the companies' balance sheet headings expressed as percentages of net assets employed.

The activities of the companies are:

**A** Manufacturer

**B** Property company

**C** High street retail stores group

**D** Multi-national with various activities

**E** Utility

**F** House building contractor.

The assets and current liabilities shown as a percentage of net assets employed are:

| | 1 % | 2 % | 3 % | 4 % | 5 % | 6 % |
|---|---|---|---|---|---|---|
| Land and buildings | 41 | 18 | 21 | 81 | 33 | 168 |
| Other fixed assets | 28 | 36 | 85 | 6 | 22 | 3 |
| Stock and work in progress | 33 | 45 | 8 | 23 | 80 | - |
| Debtors | 36 | 56 | 40 | 1 | 4 | 7 |
| Cash and bank | 5 | 3 | 5 | 17 | 1 | - |
| | 143 | 158 | 159 | 128 | 140 | 178 |
| Creditors | (34) | (47) | (21) | (28) | (29) | (9) |
| Bank overdraft/loans | (9) | (11) | (38) | (-) | (11) | (69) |
| Net assets employed | 100 | 100 | 100 | 100 | 100 | 100 |

**Question:**

Which balance sheet profile relates to the appropriate company activity?

**Answer:**

**Companies 1 and 2** – a similar balanced mix of land and building, other fixed assets, stocks, debtors and creditors. These could both be typical traditional manufacturing/ engineering companies or the multi-national which, with its various activities, would take on an 'average' profile.

**Company 1** – is taken to be the multi-national and **Company 2** – the manufacturing company (although similar to 1, company 2 has other higher fixed assets (equipment), stock, debtors and creditors which would fit with the nature of a traditional manufacturing business).

**Company 3** – fixed assets are high in total and there are other very high fixed assets, eg plant and equipment. There is also a high level of debtors. These facts alone would indicate that this might be the utility. Further there is a fairly high level of loans, again typical of a utility's balance sheet with its fixed assets available as security for the high level of borrowings.

**Company 4** – High Street retail stores – a high percentage of worth is in land and buildings with other lower fixed assets eg fixtures and fittings. Retail stocks should not be high and it is unlikely that there will be significant debtors.

**Company 5** – house building contractor – the principal assets will be work in progress – other assets/creditors will be insignificant.

**Company 6** – property company – the principal assets must be land and buildings – other assets/creditors will be insignificant.

## Checklist

✓ A balance sheet is at a specific date.

✓ A balance sheet has two sides:

- what the business owns net
- and who owns/funds it.

✓ Balance sheets should reflect the nature of the business.

# chapter one

section two

## Balance sheets

Balance sheets: structure and contents – UK

Interpreting the balance sheet

Balance sheets: structure and contents – US

Checklist

# Balance sheets structure and contents – UK

## Further definitions

Fixed assets were defined in Section 1 as assets held for long-term use and normally not traded on a regular basis. The term 'fixed asset' is commonly used in respect of physical, tangible assets. However, businesses may have three types of fixed asset, that is, long-term assets, and the following terms are used.

### *Tangible fixed assets*

These are physical, real, tangible assets – land and buildings, equipment and fixtures and fittings.

### *Intangible fixed assets*

These are not normally physical, tangible assets but are of value to the business or are necessary for the business's trade to function. Examples are patent, know-how, brand names and goodwill.

### *Investment fixed assets*

These are investments in other companies, partnerships or ventures held on a long-term basis. Examples are share holdings in other companies, investments in joint ventures or partnerships.

### *Provisions for liabilities and charges*

These are long-term liabilities of the business.

### *Called up share capital*

This is the paid up share capital of the business in £s – the value of each share may be in units other than £s, eg 20p shares.

### *Share premium account*

When a company, particularly an established company, issues more shares, it is unlikely that the value of each share will be the face value. If the business prospects are good a 20p share may well sell for 50p. The called up share capital is the face value (in £s) of the shares issued, therefore the premium (30p per share in this example) has to be credited to a share premium account.

### Revaluation reserve

If fixed assets are revalued there is a profit arising on the revaluation and this amount is credited to the revaluation reserve.This is an unrealised profit - there is no cash inflow to back it - and is thus legally and practically a non-distributable reserve.

### Equity

The shareholders' funds - this is the 'risk' capital invested as ordinary shares and retained profits.The entire amounts belong to the shareholders without restriction and are at risk should the company run into trouble.

### Goodwill

The premium paid for net assets acquired (tangible, intangible and current), that is, the amount paid in excess of the book amounts of the net assets.

### Minority interests

If one company owns shares in another, it is common for the share holding to be 100%. However, this is not always the case. When a set of accounts of a group of companies is consolidated, all fixed and current assets less liabilities are consolidated or aggregated together as even with, say, a 55% share holding the group controls all the assets.The ownership of the 45% (in this example) share of net assets of the subsidiary is recognised as one figure in £s, being the minority interest in the group's net assets.

## Interpreting the balance sheet

### Working capital and gearing ratios

A manager must ensure that the organisation is able to meet its obligations as they mature. Because investing in fixed assets and stock and allowing extended credit to debtors all use cash, the manager must ensure that these uses of the cash resources are controlled and that sufficient will be available to pay creditors. Liquidity ratios attempt to measure a company's ability to meet its short-term obligations as they fall due.

### Current ratio

$$\frac{\text{Current assets}}{\text{Current liabilities}}$$

The current ratio is calculated by dividing current assets by current liabilities. Current assets are cash and assets expected to be converted into cash within one year; current liabilities are those that must be paid within one year. A company is in a good position to meet its current obligations if current assets exceed current liabilities.

Textbooks traditionally quoted this ratio as having to be 2:1 or better if a company was to be sound and able to pay its way. This might be true for a small business but larger companies have ratios of less than 2:1 and are still able to meet their debts when they fall due.

### Liquidity ratio/quick ratio/acid test ratio

$$\frac{\text{Current assets - stock or WIP}}{\text{Current liabilities}}$$

Current assets include stock/WIP which is sometimes slow-moving and not so readily converted into cash as is implied by the current ratio.The liquidity ratio therefore takes stock out of the numerator, thus providing a more rigorous test of the company's ability to settle its obligations as they fall due.

Textbooks traditionally quoted this ratio as having to be 1:1 or better if a company was to survive! That is, its cash like assets (debtors and cash) must equal its current (immediately due) liabilities.There is a logic to this, but the ratio appropriate to a business will very much depend on the type of business. For example, a supermarket could survive on a ratio of much less than 1:1, whereas a manufacturer or contractor might need a ratio of 2:1 (the debtors may not be so current!).

## Gearing – gearing ratios

$$\text{The gearing ratio} = \frac{\text{Long-term loans}}{\text{Shareholders' funds + long-term loans}}$$

(Capital employed)

This is the common definition of gearing for a company and levels might be considered as follows:

**0%-20% • low gearing** – it would be expected that most companies will have some borrowings and levels up to 20% are reasonable.The company should be aware as to why it has borrowings of, say, 14%.

**20%-35% • medium gearing** – a normal level for many companies. Loans will be regularly taken out and repaid as the company invests in new asset or new business ventures. A company should be very clear as to why it has borrowings of, say, 31% – this level of gearing should not just happen!

**35%-50% • high gearing** – this level of borrowing may be more applicable to some businesses than others, eg an airline would normally be highly geared due to the very significant investment in tangible fixed assets.

Gearing of this level requires careful management.When a company is 50% + geared, the shareholders should ask, 'Whose company is it?'.The company is certainly answerable (if not owned by) the banks.

Gearing may also be expressed by:

$$\text{Debt to equity ratio} = \frac{\text{Long-term loans}}{\text{Shareholders' funds}}$$

The numbers will be of a higher order.

eg 20% gearing = 25% or, more likely, 1 to 4 debt/equity ratio, but the message conveyed by the ratio will be as for the gearing ratio.

eg

### Hotel chain balance sheet and selected notes

The overall content of the balance sheet of a plc or any company whose accounts are filed at Companies House is the same as for the small company's balance sheet shown in Section 1. However, there will possibly be more sub headings and consequently detail may be included as notes to the accounts.

As there is limited space in which to explain detail in the published accounts of a company there is a limit as to what can be gleaned from them. However, they are an essential element in understanding the financial position of a business and can also indicate matters such as liquidity and even performance - where there are comparatives.

A brief commentary on the hotel chain balance sheet and relevant notes is as follows.

## Balance sheet
*at 31 January 2xx5*

| | Notes | Group 2xx5 £ million | Group Restated 2xx4 £ million |
|---|---|---|---|
| **Fixed assets** | | | |
| Tangible assets | 12 | 4,032 | 3,783 |
| Investments | 13 | 240 | 229 |
| **Total fixed assets** | | **4,272** | **4,012** |
| **Current assets** | | | |
| Stocks | 14 | 47 | 45 |
| Debtors | 15 | 232 | 187 |
| Amount receivable from disposal of a subsidiary undertaking | | – | 155 |
| Short term deposits and cash | | 40 | 36 |
| **Total current assets** | | **319** | **423** |
| **Creditors due within one year** | | | |
| Borrowings | 17 | 70 | 248 |
| Other creditors | 16 | 480 | 366 |
| **Total current liabilities** | | **550** | **614** |
| **Net current liabilities** | | **(231)** | **(191)** |
| **Total assets less current liabilities** | | **4,041** | **3,821** |
| **Creditors due after one year** | | | |
| Convertible bonds | 17 | 90 | 90 |
| Borrowings | 17 | 982 | 897 |
| Finance lease obligations | 17,18 | 475 | 465 |
| Other creditors | 16 | 32 | 17 |
| **Total net assets** | | **2,462** | **2,352** |
| **Equity** | | | |
| Share capital | 19 | 236 | 216 |
| Share premium | 20 | 276 | 120 |
| Revaluation reserve | 20 | 1,683 | 1,674 |
| Goodwill reserve | 20 | (89) | |
| Profit and loss reserve | 20 | 269 | 256 |
| **Shareholders' investment** | | **2,375** | **2,266** |
| Minority interests | | 87 | 86 |
| **Total equity** | | **2,462** | **2,352** |

## Notes to the Accounts
*continued*

| | Land and buildings | | | | | | |
|---|---|---|---|---|---|---|---|
| | Freehold | Leasehold | | | | | |
| | | Long | Short | Plant and machinery | Furniture and equipment | Assets in course of construction | Total |
| | £ million | £ million | £ million | £ million | £ million | £ million | £ million |
| **Cost or valuation** | | | | | | | |
| At 31 January 2xx4 | **1,503** | **577** | **624** | **513** | **530** | **39** | **3,786** |
| Prior year adjustment | 330 | 116 | – | – | (16) | – | 430 |
| At 31 January 2xx4 restated | **1,833** | **693** | **624** | **513** | **514** | **39** | **4,216** |
| Currency translation differences | 4 | 1 | (3) | – | (5) | – | (3) |
| Additions | 29 | – | 31 | 28 | 41 | 31 | 160 |
| Disposals | (38) | (4) | (8) | (15) | (66) | – | (131) |
| Acquisition of subsidiaries | 118 | 27 | 41 | 7 | 31 | 1 | 225 |
| Reclassification | 16 | 4 | – | 1 | 13 | (34) | – |
| **At 31 January 2xx5** | **1,962** | **721** | **685** | **534** | **528** | **37** | **4,467** |
| **Accumulated depreciation** | | | | | | | |
| At 31 January 2xx4 | **2** | **–** | **41** | **116** | **274** | **–** | **433** |
| Currency translation differences | – | – | (2) | – | (3) | – | (5) |
| Charge for the year | – | – | 4 | 30 | 54 | – | 88 |
| Disposals | – | – | (5) | (9) | (67) | – | (81) |
| **At 31 January 2xx5** | **2** | **–** | **38** | **137** | **258** | **–** | **435** |
| **Net book amounts** | | | | | | | |
| **At 31 January 2xx5** | **1,960** | **721** | **647** | **397** | **270** | **37** | **4,032** |
| At 31 January 2xx4 | **1,831** | **693** | **583** | **397** | **240** | **39** | **3,783** |

| **Historical cost of property and fixed assets at valuation** | 2xx5<br>£ million | 2xx4<br>£ million |
|---|---|---|
| Cost – at 31 January | **2,857** | **2,226** |
| – prior year adjustment | – | 389 |
| Accumulated depreciation | (435) | (433) |
| **Historical net book amount** | **2,422** | **2,182** |

## Balance sheet notes

As at 31 January 2xx4, the hotel chain's properties were included in the accounts on the basis of professional valuations over a three year period - adjusted by the results of a supplementary review of the entire portfolio as at that date. Having consulted with the hotel chain's advisers, the Directors have concluded that the charges in market values since 31 January 2xx4 would not be sufficiently material to make a further professional valuation worthwhile at this stage.

It is intended to revalue properties on a systematic five year rolling programme, with one fifth of the portfolio being revalued each year.

At 31 January 2xx5, the company had capital expenditure commitments totalling £54m (2xx4 - £59m) of which £28m (2xx4 £29m) were committed and £26m (2xx4 - £30m) approved by the Board but not committed.

Tangible fixed assets include capitalised interest of £52m (2xx4 - £54m). The prior year adjustment relates to the adoption of FRS5 (Note 18). Firstly, as was stated in Section 1, the balance sheet should relate to the business. In other words the reader should have some knowledge of the business, at least its areas of operation. The company was a hotel and catering group which had been built up over the years by the acquisition of hotels, hotel companies and other associated activities.

The balance sheet profile for a business which was as much a property company as anything thus has significant tangible fixed assets. Note 12 to the accounts shows the details of the tangible fixed assets - a fixed asset table. In note 12 we find confirmation that the most significant part of investment in tangible fixed assets was indeed in freehold and leasehold property, with the remainder being in plant, machinery, furniture and equipment. There were also assets in course of construction - new hotels and resorts. Another very important point to note is the disclosure that the historical cost of the tangible assets was considerably less as the properties had been revalued over the years of ownership. This thus gave rise to a revaluation reserve shown under the heading 'Equity' - shareholders' funds.

The relative amounts under other balance sheet headings are also in line with the type of business.

- Low levels of stocks - food and liquor and supplies would be purchased as required - the days of holding fine wine cellars are unfortunately over - wine has to be purchased 'just in time'.

- Low levels of debtors, these comprised almost half trade debtors - account customers with the other half being pre-payments.

- Creditors falling due within one year - current liabilities were a mix of trade, taxation, sundry creditors and accruals.

- Overall there is negative working capital - really due to the low levels of stocks/low debtors but reasonable levels of current liabilities.

Creditors due after more than one year were significant, this need not be the case, the business could be financed entirely by the shareholders, but as there is the excellent security in the properties owned, it is almost inevitable that such a business will have considerable borrowings and be highly geared.

Regarding equity, the most significant figure was the revaluation reserve - it was the ownership of the valuable properties which gave the shareholders' worth. It is also interesting to note that the Profit and Loss reserve - retained profit figure was not very high in relation to total equity. Either the company had not made large profits over the years or it had a history of paying out the profits as dividends.

## Balance sheets: structure and contents – US

The first point to note with a US balance sheet is that it will be laid out in what we would consider to be an old fashioned style. That is, there is firstly a listing of assets (current then fixed) which is totalled. This is followed by a listing of liabilities (current and long-term) and liabilities to shareholders. These are then totalled.

This layout is very traditional and goes back to the time when the balance sheet's prime purpose was as a control statement, that is, the total assets and liabilities of the business were listed, the totals then should agree, giving some comfort that at the end of a period, business assets and liabilities were complete and correctly accounted for – basically it was a trial balance (see Chapter 4).

### Further definitions

*Cash equivalents or liquid resources*

Current asset investments held as readily disposable stores of value.

*Accounts receivable*

American for trade debtors.

*Inventories*

American for stocks and work in progress.

*Account payable*

Trade creditors payable within 12 months.

## Oil corporation consolidated balance sheet and selected notes

Firstly, as was stated in Section 1, the balance sheet should relate to the business. In other words, the reader should have some knowledge of the business, at least its areas of operation. This corporation is one of the oil majors, owning mineral rights and is an oil exploration and processing company.

As with earlier examples the relevant amounts under each balance sheet heading should relate to the business activities carried out.

Firstly, note that the US balance sheet is a list of assets, in a decreasing order of realisation as you go down the page, that is, cash and liquid assets are shown first and fixed, long-term assets last. This is followed by a list of liabilities to both third parties and to shareholders - equity. The order of display again tends to start with short-term or current liabilities through to the long-term.

## Comments on the oil corporation's balance sheet

Cash and marketable securities - the oil industry is about oil and cash - $s, and therefore it is no surprise that there is a high level of cash.

There are considerable amounts in inventories (stocks) crude oil and products being the major heading.

The greatest part of investment in assets is in tangible fixed assets - property, plant and equipment. There is also a material amount invested in intangible assets.

At this point it is worth noting that whilst US based companies or their subsidiaries have to file voluminous detail with the Securities Exchange Commission (SEC) there is generally less detail in US accounts than would be found in UK accounts.

## Consolidated balance sheet

| | Dec. 31 2xx5 | Dec. 31 2xx4 |
|---|---|---|
| | *(millions of dollars)* | |
| **Assets** | | |
| Current assets | | |
| Cash and cash equivalents | $1,508 | $1,157 |
| Other marketable securities | 281 | 618 |
| Notes and accounts receivable, less estimated doubtful amounts | 8,925 | 8,073 |
| Inventories | | |
| Crude oil, products and merchandise | 4,865 | 4,717 |
| Materials and supplies | 816 | 824 |
| Prepaid taxes and expenses | 923 | 1,071 |
| Total current assets | $17,318 | $16,460 |
| Investments and advances | 5,697 | 5,394 |
| Property, plant and equipment, at cost, less accumulated depreciation and depletion | 65,446 | 63,425 |
| Other assets, including intangibles, net | 2,835 | 2,583 |
| **Total assets** | **$91,296** | **$87,862** |
| **Liabilities** | | |
| Current liabilities | | |
| Notes and loans payable | $2,247$ | 3,858 |
| Accounts payable and accrued liabilities | 14,113 | 13,391 |
| Income taxes payable | 2,376 | 2,244 |
| Total current liabilities | $18,736 | $19,493 |
| Long-term debt | 7,778 | 8,831 |
| Annuity reserves and accrued liabilities | 8,770 | 7,792 |
| Deferred income tax liabilities | 12,431 | 11,435 |
| Deferred credits | 975 | 728 |
| Equity of minority and preferred shareholders in affiliated companies | 2,170 | 2,168 |
| **Total liabilities** | **$50,860** | **$50,447** |
| **Shareholders' Equity** | | |
| Preferred stock without par value (authorised 200 million shares) | $454 | $554 |
| Guaranteed LESOP obligation | (501) | (613) |
| Common stock without par value (authorised 2 billion shares,1,813 million issued) | 2,822 | 2,822 |
| Earnings reinvested | 53,539 | 50,821 |
| Cumulative foreign exchange translation adjustment | 1,339 | 848 |
| Common stock held in treasury (571 million shares in 2xx5 and 2xx4) | (17,217) | (17,017) |
| Total shareholders' equity | $40,436 | $37,415 |
| Total liabilities and shareholders' equity | $91,296 | $87,862 |

***The information on pages F11 through F20 is an integral part of these statements.***

In this corporation's balance sheet there are no references to notes on figures in the balance sheet. Pages F11 through to F20 are an integral part of the statements and do contain further explanation of the background to some figures rather than an analysis. As an example, note 3 on F12 of the Annual Report is as follows:

> **Cash flow information**
>
> The consolidated statement of cash flows provides information about changes in cash and cash equivalents. All short-term marketable securities, with original maturities of three months or less, that are readily convertible to known amounts of cash and are so near maturity that they present insignificant risk of changes in interest rates, are classified as cash equivalents.

Accounts payable is a significant current liability and this probably follows from the size and commercial strength of the oil corporation as much as anything - their suppliers will be happy to wait!

There is a substantial amount in annuity reserves and accrued liabilities and the note on F indicates what this figure is, as well as showing the US style of notes to accounts - they are more discursive in form rather than analytical.

Under shareholders' equity common stock without par value are the shares of the company traded on stock markets.

The most significant figure under shareholders' equity is the earnings reinvested - indicating the historical profitability of the company.

Common stock held in treasury is stock of the company repurchased by the company.

In Chapter 6 Section 2 on Interpretation of the figures the above balance sheet is analysed into a form more suited for management purposes, showing the net capital employed on one side with shareholders' equity and long-term finance on the other.

g

*Interpretation of balance sheets*

To recap on the introductory points on interpretation of any financial statements:

**The financial statement should reflect the activities and position of the business being accounted for and reviewed.**

**With your knowledge of the business look for obvious, significant types of assets/liabilities and their respective amounts in the balance sheet.**

The following illustrations are examples of what is meant by the above guidance:

**A** a balance sheet of a new small business

**B** the balance sheet of British Telecoms plc

**A balance sheet for a small company** set up two years ago by a husband and wife, using nearly 100,000 of retirement pension funds to invest in and operate a small country hotel. The remainder of the 250,000 plus funding was to come from bank, HP loans and an overdraft.

**Small company balance sheet**
*as at (a date)*

| | | | |
|---|---|---|---|
| **Fixed assets** | Land and buildings | 250,000 | |
| | Fixtures and fittings | 23,500 | |
| | Motor vehicles | 15,500 | |
| | | | **289,000** |
| **Current assets** | Stock | 6,700 | |
| | Debtors | 12,300 | |
| | Cash | 200 | |
| | | 19,200 | |
| **Current liabilities** | Overdraft | 7,200 | |
| | Trade creditors | 13,400 | |
| | Current portion of loans | | 5,000 |
| | PAYE/NIC | 2,100 | |
| | | 27,700 | |
| | Net current liabilities | | (8,500) |
| | | | **280,500** |
| **Shareholders' funds** | Called up share capital | 100,000 | |
| | Profit and loss account | 14,900 | |
| | | | 114,900 |
| **Long-term liabilities** (Creditors: amounts falling due after more than one year) | | | |
| | Loan on property | 140,000 | |
| | HP loans | 25,600 | |
| | | | 165,600 |
| | | | **280,500** |

Of course you would need to know the cost of the property, the exact amount of borrowings, the cost of the fixtures and fittings, levels of stock (liquor) etc, but this only indicates the second vital knowledge required to interpret financial statements - there has to be as detailed a knowledge of the business as possible. This means its size, location, business processes, employee numbers etc. This is of course the very information which many managers know about their businesses - more than the accountant knows!

With knowledge of the business and the understanding that the figures should represent the form of the business being displayed in the financial statements, the balance sheet should confirm the understanding or reveal potential areas of doubt about the business operation (or of course, careless, negligent or deliberate errors in the figures!). *See over.*

## Balance sheet of a telecommunication company plc

*at 31 March 2xx7*

| | Notes | 2xx7 £ million | 2xx6 £ million |
|---|---|---|---|
| **Fixed assets** | | | |
| Tangible assets | *11* | **16,802** | 16,496 |
| Investments | *12* | **1,273** | 1,057 |
| **Total fixed assets** | | **18,075** | 17,553 |
| | | | |
| **Current assets** | | | |
| Stocks | | **180** | 212 |
| Debtors | *13* | **3,807** | 3,082 |
| Investments | *14* | **2,974** | 2,568 |
| Cash at bank and in hand | | **26** | 121 |
| Total current assets | | **6,987** | 5,983 |
| **Creditors: amounts falling due within one year** | | | |
| Loans and other borrowings | *15* | **483** | 315 |
| Other creditors | *16* | **9,171** | 5,774 |
| **Total creditors: amounts falling due within one year** | | **9,654** | 6,089 |
| | | | |
| **Net current liabilities** | | **(2,667)** | (106) |
| Total assets less current liabilities | | **15,408** | 17,447 |
| | | | |
| **Creditors: amounts falling due after more than one year** | | | |
| Loans and other borrowings | *15* | **2,693** | 3,322 |
| | | | |
| **Provisions for liabilities and charges** | *17* | **1,391** | 1,267 |
| | | | |
| **Minority interests** | | **208** | 180 |
| | | | |
| **Capital and reserves** | | | |
| Called up share capital | *18* | **1,589** | 1,573 |
| Share premium account | *19* | **675** | 531 |
| Other reserves | *19* | **777** | 777 |
| Profit and loss account | *19* | **8,075** | 9,797 |
| **Total equity shareholders' funds** | *20* | **11,116** | 12,678 |
| | | **15,408** | 17,447 |

***Debtors include amounts receivable after more than one year of £546m (2xx6 – £87m).***

## 11. Tangible fixed assets

| | Land and buildings (*a*) £ million | Plant and equipment £ million | Assets in course of construction £ million | Total £ million |
|---|---|---|---|---|
| **Group** | | | | |
| **Cost** | | | | |
| Balances at 1 April 2xx6 | 2,763 | 27,586 | 1,001 | 31,350 |
| Acquisitions of subsidiary undertakings | – | 11 | – | 11 |
| Additions | 14 | 849 | 1,884 | 2,747 |
| Transfers | 99 | 1,774 | (1,873) | – |
| Disposals and adjustments | (75) | (1,014) | (33) | (1,122) |
| **Total cost at 31 March 2xx7** | **2,801** | **29,206** | **979** | **32,986** |
| **Depreciation** | | | | |
| Balances at 1 April 2xx6 | 1,258 | 13,708 | – | 14,966 |
| Acquisitions of subsidiary undertakings | – | 2 | – | 2 |
| Charge for the year | 109 | 2,156 | – | 2,265 |
| Disposals and adjustments | (51) | (914) | – | (965) |
| **Total depreciation at 31 March 2xx7** | **1,316** | **14,952** | **–** | **16,268** |
| **Net book value at 31 March 2xx7** | 1,485 | 14,254 | 979 | 16,718 |
| Engineering stores | – | – | 84 | 84 |
| **Total tangible fixed assets at 31 March 2xx7** | **1,485** | **14,254** | **1,063** | **16,802** |
| Net book value at 31 March 2xx6 | 1,505 | 13,878 | 1,001 | 16,384 |
| Engineering stores | – | – | 112 | 112 |
| Total tangible fixed assets at 31 March 2xx6 | 1,505 | 13,878 | 1,113 | 16,496 |

## 16. Other creditors

| | Group | | Company | |
|---|---|---|---|---|
| | **2xx7 £ million** | **2xx6 £ million** | **2xx7 £ million** | **2xx6 £ million** |
| Trade creditors | **1,858** | 1,732 | **1,483** | 1,455 |
| Amounts owed to subsidiary undertakings | **–** | – | **898** | 726 |
| Amounts owed to associated undertakings | **46** | 37 | **–** | 2 |
| Corporation taxes | **1,774** | 1,091 | **1,503** | 1,007 |
| Other taxation and social security | **332** | 354 | **321** | 359 |
| Other creditors | **1,134** | 853 | **931** | 701 |
| Accrued expenses | **313** | 282 | **203** | 168 |
| Deferred income | **706** | 710 | **658** | 685 |
| Dividends (*a*) | **3,008** | 715 | **3,008** | 715 |
| Total other creditors | **9,171** | 5,774 | **9,005** | 5,818 |
| Total other creditors included amounts due after more than one year: | | | | |
| Deferred income | **13** | 28 | **13** | 28 |

(*a*) The 2xx7 figures include the special dividend of £2,244m.

## Commentary on a telecommunication company balance sheet

The figures from the company's balance sheet have in fact already been commented upon in Section 1, where the profile of the company's balance sheet in percentage terms was given.The basic points to consider when looking at the balance sheet of a utility would be the following:

How large are the **tangible fixed assets**? You would expect a utility to have large amounts of assets/infrastructure. It is relevant to know the basis on which the assets are valued. Is this at depreciated historical cost (for equipment), or revalued amounts (land and property). Do the depreciation rates seem reasonable? How old are the assets? This can be deduced from the size of the accumulated depreciation with respect to the cost of the assets. Most of this information will be found in the notes to the accounts and for the telecommunication company the relevant note 11 is given on the page following the balance sheet.

Does the company have other fixed assets? In this company's case there are considerable **investments** in operating subsidiaries, or set up to expand the business into new areas as telecoms markets world-wide become liberalised.

**Current assets** – relative to total capital employed stocks should be a low figure and this is indeed the case. For a utility offering as much as three months' credit on billing trade debtors will probably be quite high and again this is the case for this particular company.Whether or not there are cash, bank or short-term investment balances is very much related to how funds are managed in the company, also there may have been a recent sale of assets, or funds may be accumulated short-term for imminent expansion, investment in new tangible or investment fixed assets.

**Creditors: amounts falling due within one year** – as with any large respected company, with its size and economic strength it is quite likely to be able to dictate payment terms and command a high level of short-term borrowing. Detail of other creditors may be found in note 16. On analysis, trade creditors are a significant figure, as is corporation tax payable. Finally the proposed dividend, along with a special dividend amounts to nearly one third of current liabilities.

A figure for **total assets less current liabilities** is shown 15,408 for 2xx7. This is the capital employed by them. The telecommunication company are unusual in that this is where they 'draw the line'. Most UK companies go on to deduct the long-term creditors - amounts falling due after more than one year, although the Companies Act does not specifically require this approach. The company's approach is really far more helpful as it shows capital employed on one 'side' of the balance sheet and capital (equity and loans) invested on the other.

The telecommunication company's balance sheet goes on to show **creditors: amounts falling due after more than one year**, being loans and other borrowings, provisions for liabilities and charges and minority interests. As might be expected of a utility with significant cash generating tangible fixed assets as security, they have considerable borrowings - gearing of 2,693/15,408 = 17.5% assuming that provisions for liabilities and charges are not imminently payable liabilities and wholly or partly long-term funding. Although gearing on the basis described above is reasonable, the question might be raised as to why gearing is not higher. A sound company (as is the example given) ought to be able to borrow at competitive rates and loan interest should be lower than the effective rates demanded by shareholders/ the market.

**Capital and reserves** - shareholders' equity comprises the called up share capital and share premium, indicating the shares have been sold at a premium to their par value. Other reserves are principally capital redemption reserve, a reserve required by law where the company has purchased its own shares. The existence of this reserve may imply that the company is doing the right thing by buying its own shares with its own cash and in effect distributing the funds to shareholders - the share price goes up if there are fewer shares. Shareholders may then sell shares if they wish. It is often considered better to give cash back to shareholders in this way or by means of higher (or special dividends) rather than the company hang on to the cash and maybe invest it unwisely.

Profit and loss accounts - a significant balance indicating a history of profit making and a company which has reinvested in the business.

The total of creditors: amounts falling due after more than one year and capital and reserves is 15,408, the capital invested in the business and of course equal to the capital employed figure.

## Interpretation of balance sheets for specific purposes

The above points on interpretation cover a general understanding of what a balance sheet may reveal or confirm about a business. A further very important, obvious, but often overlooked issue when interpreting financial statements is that there must be a reason for looking at the figures. Have you ever looked at your month end reports - whatever they may be - and said to yourself (or aloud) 'Why am I looking at these?'

There has to be clear reason or a remit when interpreting figures. For example, you could look at a balance sheet to consider the worth or value of a business, you could look at a balance sheet from the view of a bank who might lend money, you could look at the balance sheet's disposition and amounts of individual assets/liabilities with a view to bench marking and considering the efficient use of assets.

## 'Window dressing'

Whilst detailed individual balances cannot be changed (unless there is fraud!) it may be possible to net two or more figures, sub-divide balances 'gross up' two figures which have been correctly netted, reposition balances, or enter into transactions before the year end and reverse them after the year end, all with the purpose of changing the form and emphasis of the balance sheet. UK Accounting Standard 17.10 indicates to accountants and auditors that potential for the last form of window dressing should be considered, any material cases identified and the position reversed to show the correct or fair position at the balance sheet date. Other Accounting Standards and good practice consider most forms of window dressing unacceptable.

## Checklist

- ✓ Balance sheets can have different structures and use different terminology.
- ✓ Balance sheet terms and structures can be aligned.
- ✓ Balance sheets should reflect the nature of the business.
- ✓ Manipulation (window dressing) of balance sheet structures may be possible.

# chapter two

section one

## Profit and loss accounts

What is a profit and loss account?

What do profit and loss accounts reveal about a business?

Checklist

## What is a profit and loss account?

A profit and loss account is a statement of sales less costs for a period, normally one year or sub-periods thereof. It shows sales (also called turnover, income or revenue) less costs (or expenses) grouped in various ways, the end result being the net profit of the business.

### A simple P & L account

In its most simple format a profit and loss account starts with sales or income from which all costs or expenses are deducted and the net result is a profit, if costs are less than sales or a loss if costs exceed sales.

**Sales (turnover, income or revenue)** arise from supplying goods and services to customers. Such supplies are recorded as sales whether or not they have actually been paid for, sales figures thus include sales on credit.

**Costs or expenses** arise from the purchase of goods or services onward for sale to customers plus all necessary costs incurred for the period.

*Profit and loss account for the period ended...*

| | |
|---|---|
| **Sales or income** | **700** |
| – | |
| **Costs or expenses** | **(660)** |
| = | |
| **Net profit or (loss)** | **40** |

In accounting terms, a profit or loss is the result of deducting all costs from all income for a defined time period. Whilst this is in essence a very simple concept and thus statement, it will be obvious that the correct inclusion of income and costs is critical from the point of view of timing.

A very common practice is to distinguish between costs of purchased items, costs of manufacturing or direct costs of providing a service and the general, indirect or overhead costs of running a business.

*Profit and loss account for the period ended...*

| | |
|---|---|
| **Sales/turnover/ revenue** | **700** |
| – | |
| **Cost of sales** | **(500)** |
| = | |
| **Gross profit** | **200** |
| – | |
| **Expenses/overheads** (grouped together either for management purposes or to meet statutory requirements) | **(160)** |
| = | |
| **Net profit before tax** | **40** |

## P & L account – definition of terms

*Sales/turnover/revenue/income*

This is the total sales invoiced by a business during the period the profit and loss account covers. It should exclude VAT or similar taxes as these are not income of the business but amounts collected on behalf of the tax authorities.

*Cost of sales*

This should be the direct costs of the services provided or goods supplied: eg for a consultancy firm the cost of salaries; for a retailer the cost of merchandise at purchase price.

In management accounts, cost of sales and thus the resultant gross profit, should be clear and unambiguous and this is normally the case. In published accounts, since there is no statutory definition of cost of sales, companies tend to obscure their true gross profits by adding in overhead costs and other expenses.

*Gross profit*

This is the difference between sales and the cost of sales. Its importance is as a performance and control measure.The accuracy and worth of the measure thus depends on clear and consistent definition of cost of sales.

*Expenses*

This is a heading for all other costs, but other terms may be used, eg overheads or the expenses split and grouped - employment costs, office or occupancy costs, finance costs, etc.

On the following page there is a profit and loss account for a simple business:

eg

**Simple Business**

*Profit and loss account for the year ended 31 March 2xx6*

| | | | |
|---|---|---|---|
| **Sales** | | | 201,000 |
| **Cost of sales** | Stock at beginning of year | 20,400 | |
| | Purchases during year | 107,200 | |
| | | 127,600 | |
| | Stock at end of year | (22,500) | |
| | | | 105,100 |
| **Gross profit margin** | | | 95,900 |
| **Expenses** | Wages | 51,200 | |
| | Rent and rates | 6,100 | |
| | Heat and light | 1,900 | |
| | Stationery/postage | 1,300 | |
| | Insurance | 1,200 | |
| | Advertising | 900 | |
| | Interest payable | 1,400 | |
| | Depreciation | 3,800 | |
| | | | 67,800 |
| **Net profit before tax** | | | 28,100 |
| **Taxation** | | | 7,500 |
| **Net profit for year** | | | 20,600 |

The P & L account on the previous page is for a small trading company and for the size of business the layout is probably quite adequate. However, it should be appreciated that profit and loss figures, particularly the expenses, can be grouped in any manner which assists in understanding and thus managing the business. It should also be noted that in the UK and other countries there may be statutory requirements in respect of how P & L expenses are grouped (see Section 2).

As an illustration of what is meant, for the above simple example it might be helpful to the business owner/manager to group the expenses as follows:

eg

| | | | |
|---|---|---|---|
| **Gross profit margin** | | | 95,900 |
| **Expenses** | | | |
| **Labour** | | | |
| Wages | 51,200 | | |
| | | 51,200 | |
| **Occupancy** | | | |
| Rent and rates | 6,100 | | |
| Heat and light | 1,900 | | |
| Insurance | 1,200 | | |
| Depreciation | 3,800 | | |
| | | 13,000 | |
| **Administration** | | | |
| Stationery /postage | 1,300 | | |
| Advertising | 900 | | |
| | | 2,200 | |
| **Finance costs** | | | |
| Interest Payable | 1,400 | | |
| | | 1,400 | |
| | | | 67,800 |
| **Net profit before tax** | | | 28,100 |

## What do profit and loss accounts reveal about a business?

There are endless possibilities regarding the analysis of expenditure, the overriding principal should be to have the minimum necessary to be able to properly manage the business.

The first point to remember when interpreting any financial statements is that the figures are not the creation of an accountant, but should represent the business for which they are prepared. Careless record keeping (book keeping), inappropriate and inconsistent rules (accounting policies) or deliberate miss statement (fraud!) may of course give unreliable statements, but it is assumed that the reader is dealing with reliable statements.

Probably the most important use of profit and loss accounts is in the identifying of trends – hopefully growth in sales, control of costs and maximisation of profit.

The following illustration is an example of what is meant by the above assertion that the P & L account should represent the business for which it has been prepared:

The profit and loss accounts overleaf, with gross profit and costs expressed as percentages of sales, are of three different types of business.

g

**P** - a manufacturer; **Q** - an hotel and **R** - a retailer.

| | | **P** | **Q** | **R** |
|---|---|---|---|---|
| Sales | | 100% | 100% | 100% |
| Cost of sales | Materials | 22% | 14% | 51% |
| | Wages/salaries | 20% | 21% | 0% |
| | Overhead | 13% | 0% | 0% |
| | Depreciation | 15% | 0% | 0% |
| Gross profit | | 30% | 65% | 49% |
| Wages/salaries | | 8% | 9% | 17% |
| Occupancy | | 4% | 21% | 14% |
| Administration | | 6% | 13% | 5% |
| Depreciation | | 2% | 12% | 3% |
| Total costs | | 20% | 55% | 39% |
| **Operating profit** | | 10% | 10% | 10% |

The above figures are for small businesses and whilst a more detailed description of their activities would assist in comprehending the figures, at this stage the point is being made that as with a balance sheet (1.1) or for any report with figures, the figures should be of the business described and not just the creation of a bookkeeper or accountant.

The headings against which figures are disclosed, as well as the size of the number is very important when analysing figures. In this example the manufacturer will have sizeable material and wage costs as part of the cost of manufacture - cost of sales. A hotelier might consider only the costs of staff and bought in food, liquor and other consumables as being cost of sales. A retailer will normally consider the cost of sales to comprise solely the cost of bought in merchandise for retail. Further discussion of what may be included in cost of sales is included in Section 2.

The overall interpretation of the figures is as follows:

The manufacturer P has considerable costs in materials, wages and depreciation as would be expected. General expenses, wages, occupancy, administration costs and office depreciation are relatively low.

The hotel Q has considerable staff costs, with noticeably high occupancy costs.

The retailer R has cost of sales comprising only materials - merchandise bought in for resale, staff and occupancy costs are the only other material expenses.

The point of the above analysis is not that you could instantly identify a business from the P & L account structure, but rather that the headings and amounts found in a P & L account will relate to the business being reviewed.

Hopefully the above matching appears reasonable to the reader, it is obviously easy to do this exercise with knowledge of the answer! The point with interpretation of figures is that information should be used to firstly identify key figures. Once key figures are understood and matched, the remainder should fall in place.

There is a review question with feedback solution which may be used to enhance you interpretation skills and develop an understanding of profit and loss account structure. Also in the second section interpretation of profit and loss accounts is covered in much more detail.

## Interpreting profit and loss account profiles

**Question:**

Set out below are the principal activities of four companies, together with information from the companies' Profit and Loss Accounts with costs expressed as percentages of sales.

The respective areas of activity of the companies are:

1 Telecoms utility

2 Food retailer

3 Coal mining company

4 Hotel group

Costs as a percentage of sales are:

| | P | Q | R | S |
|---|---|---|---|---|
| Sales | 100% | 100% | 100% | 100% |
| Cost of sales/ materials | 33% | 11% | 24% | 54% |
| Staff costs | 24% | 20% | 28% | 10% |
| Depreciation | 18% | 25% | 7% | 5% |
| Other operating costs | 14% | 25% | 21% | 22% |
| Research and development | 0% | 2% | 0% | 0% |
| Finance costs | 2% | 1% | 8% | 0% |
| **Operating profit** | 9% | 16% | 12% | 9% |

## Interpreting profit and loss account profiles – feedback

As with any interpretation of figures there are two ways of approaching the task:

> does the knowledge of the business or activity under review indicate a particular format or profile for the figures?

*and*

> do the figures have any particular profile or attributes?

In this example it is worth considering what the profile of costs might be for the business types given:

### 1 *Telecoms utility*

Cost of sales/materials....... relatively low costs of operating
Staff costs .......... medium
Depreciation.......... high – a lot of equipment
Other operating costs .......... low
Research and development .......... some
Finance costs.......... could have high borrowings

### 2 *Food retailer*

Cost of sales/materials.......... maybe 40%-50% of sales
Staff costs .......... medium
Depreciation .......... fairly low
Other operating costs .......... medium
Research and development.......... none
Finance costs.......... low – a cash generating business

### 3 *Coal mining company*

Cost of sales/materials .......... medium
Staff costs .......... medium
Depreciation.......... fairly high – a lot of equipment
Other operating costs.......... fairly low if a site office
Research and development.......... possible
Finance costs .......... low, medium or high

*4 Hotel group*

Cost of sales/materials ..................... medium

Staff costs ..................... high

Depreciation ..................... low – property rather than equipment

Other operating costs ..................... medium

Research and development ..................... none

Finance costs ..................... could be highly geared – property loans

*The best fit for the above profiles is:*

| | |
|---|---|
| Telecoms | Q |
| Food retailer | S |
| Mining company | P |
| Hotel group | R |

## Checklist

- ✓ P & L account profiles should relate to the business.
- ✓ P & L gross profit/margins should relate to the business.
- ✓ P & L costs as % of sales should relate to the business.

# chapter two

section two

## Profit and loss accounts

Profit and loss accounts in published or statutory accounts

US revenue or income statement (P & L account) structure and contents

Checklist

## Profit and loss accounts in published or statutory accounts

There is really a very limited amount of detail which has to be disclosed in the accounts for shareholders, or those which have to be filed at Companies House.

Taking the simple P & L account shown in Section 1, the most common disclosure layout to be found in published accounts is shown on the following page. To illustrate what a published P & L account may reveal, comparative figures for 2xx5 have been included. Also calculation of costs, profits etc, as percentages of sales - note that this is not required in published accounts.

The information which has to be disclosed is: sales, or more commonly turnover; cost of sales; gross profit and then other expenses or overheads grouped as administration costs, with depreciation shown separately; operating profit; interest payable or receivable; profit before tax; taxation; profit after tax (available for shareholders); dividends paid or proposed; and finally, profit retained.

The full list of possible headings is given in the formats shown in Schedule 5 to the Companies Act 1985.

**P & L account for the year ended**

| | | 2xx6 | as a % of sales | | 2xx5 | as a % of sales |
|---|---|---|---|---|---|---|
| Sales | | 201,000 | | | 198,000 | |
| Cost of sales | | (105,100) | 52% | | (102,400) | 52% |
| Gross profit | | 95,900 | 48% | | 95,600 | 48% |
| admin costs | (62,600) | | 31% | (58,700) | | 30% |
| depreciation | (3,800) | | 2% | (1,600) | | 1% |
| | | (66,400) | 33% | | (60,300) | 30% |
| Operating profit | | 29,500 | 15% | | 35,300 | 18% |
| Interest charge | | (1,400) | 1% | | (1,150) | 1% |
| Profit before tax | | 28,100 | 14% | | 34,150 | 17% |
| Taxation | | (7,500) | 4% | | (9,200) | 5% |
| Profit after tax | | 20,600 | 10% | | 24,950 | 13% |
| Dividend paid | | (2,000) | 1% | | (18,000) | 9% |
| Profit retained | | 18,600 | 9% | | 6,950 | 4% |

There is additional disclosure required regarding: analysis of turnover, directors' emoluments (really total of salary and other payments to them), employee remuneration, audit and other fees paid to the auditors. The extent of disclosure depends on the size of the company and for small and medium companies less disclosure is required. Full details of company classification and disclosure requirements can be found in any accounts preparation checklist.

This information is normally relegated to the notes to the accounts.

**There follows an example: the hotel chain's P & L account with selected notes.**

## Consolidated profit and loss account

*For the year ended 31 January 2xx5*

| | Notes | 2xx5 Total £ million | Restated 2xx4 Before exceptional items £ million | Restated 2xx4 Exceptional items £ million | Restated 2xx4 Total £ million | Growth before exceptional items |
|---|---|---|---|---|---|---|
| **Sales** | | | | | | |
| **Continuing operations** | | | | | | |
| Comparable | | **1,753** | **1,638** | – | **1,638** | 7% |
| Acquisitions | | 36 | – | – | – | |
| | | **1,789** | **1,638** | – | **1,638** | 9% |
| **Discontinued operations** | | – | 468 | – | 468 | |
| **Sales** | 2 | **1,789** | **2,106** | – | **2,106** | |
| Net operating costs | 3 | (1,531) | (1,881) | – | (1,881) | |
| **Operating profit** | | | | | | |
| **Continuing operations** | | | | | | |
| Comparable | | 263 | 203 | – | 203 | |
| Acquisitions – net of reorganisation costs | 2 | (5) | – | – | – | |
| | | **258** | **203** | – | **203** | 27% |
| **Discontinued operations** | | – | 22 | – | 22 | |
| **Total operating profit** | 2 | **258** | **225** | – | **225** | |
| Disposal losses and provisions on property and fixed assets | 6 | – | – | (88) | (88) | |
| Profit on disposal of discontinued operations | 6 | – | – | 122 | 122 | |
| **Profit before interest and taxation** | | **258** | **225** | **34** | **259** | 15% |
| Interest and other financing charges | 7 | (131) | (148) | – | (148) | |
| **Profit on ordinary activities before taxation** | | **127** | **77** | **34** | **111** | 65% |
| Taxation | 8 | (30) | (22) | (5) | (27) | |
| **Profit on ordinary activities after taxation** | | **97** | **55** | **29** | **84** | |
| Minority interests | | (8) | | | (8) | |
| **Profit attributable to shareholders** | | **89** | | | **76** | |
| Dividends | 9 | (69) | | | (64) | |
| **Retained earnings** | 20 | **20** | | | **12** | |
| Earnings per share | 10 | **10.1p** | **5.6p** | | **9.0p** | 80% |
| Dividends per share | 9 | **7.5p** | **7.5p** | | **7.5p** | |
| Interest cover – times | | **2.0** | **1.5** | | **1.8** | |
| Dividend cover – times | 9 | **1.3** | **0.7** | | **1.2** | |

## Notes to the Accounts (continued)

### Segmental analysis of sales and profit (continued)

**Gross sales and inter-company sales**

Gross sales of other continuing operations amounted to £230m (2xx4 – £220m), comprising £143 (2xx4 – £146m) of UK inter-company sales to the hotels and restaurants businesses and £87m (2xx4 – £74m) of sales to third parties.

| **Net operating costs** | **2xx5** | **2xx4** | | |
|---|---|---|---|---|
| | **Continuing £ million** | **Continuing £ million** | **Discontinued £ million** | **Total £ million** |
| Before exceptional items: | | | | |
| Raw materials and consumables | 510 | 474 | 187 | 661 |
| Other external charges | 401 | 361 | 145 | 506 |
| Staff costs | 471 | 452 | 99 | 551 |
| Operating lease charges: | | | | |
| Property leases | 47 | 46 | 6 | 52 |
| Equipment and vehicle leases | 11 | 13 | 1 | 14 |
| Depreciation | 88 | 89 | 8 | 97 |
| Reorganisation costs | 7 | – | – | – |
| Profits on disposal of assets | (4) | – | – | – |
| | **1,531** | **1,435** | **446** | **1,881** |

Audit fees of £1,009,000 (2xx4 – £,50,000) and UK non-audit fees of £375,000 (2xx4 – £1,700,000) were paid in respect of services provided by the auditors.

| **Employees** | **2xx5 Number Thousand** | **2xx4 Number Thousand** |
|---|---|---|
| The average number of staff employed by the company during the year was: | | |
| Continuing operations: | | |
| UK full time | 22 | 21 |
| UK part time | 9 | 10 |
| Overseas full time | 9 | 10 |
| Overseas part time | 1 | 1 |
| | **41** | **42** |
| Discontinued operations | – | 8 |
| | **41** | **50** |

| The aggregate remuneration of all employees comprised: | 2xx5 Continuing £ million | 2xx4 Continuing £ million | 2xx4 Discontinued £ million | 2xx4 Total £ million |
|---|---|---|---|---|
| Wages and salaries | 419 | 399 | 88 | 487 |
| Social security costs | 55 | 50 | 10 | 60 |
| Net pension (gain)/expense | (3) | 3 | 1 | 4 |
| | **471** | **452** | **99** | **551** |

The net pension gain comprises a gain of £5m (2xx4 – change of £2m) in respect of the principal UK pension scheme and a charge of £2m (2xx4 – £2m) in respect of other schemes.

## Statement of total recognised gains and losses

*For the year ended 31 January 2xx5*

| | Notes | 2xx5 £ million | Restated 2xx4 £ million |
|---|---|---|---|
| **Profit attributable to shareholders** | | **89** | **76** |
| Unrealised deficit on revaluation of properties | | – | (324) |
| **Total gains and losses for the year before currency adjustments** | | **89** | **(248)** |
| Currency translation differences | | (2) | (72) |
| **Total recognised gains and losses for the year** | | **87** | (320) |
| Prior year adjustment | 18 | (40) | |
| **Total gains and losses recognised since last Annual Report** | | **47** | |

## Reconciliation of movements in shareholders' funds

*For the year ended 31 January 2xx5*

| | Notes | 2xx5 £ million | Restated 2xx4 £ million |
|---|---|---|---|
| **Profit attributable to shareholders** | | **89** | **76** |
| Dividends | 9 | (69) | (64) |
| **Transfer from profit and loss account** | | **20** | **12** |
| Unrealised deficit on revaluation of properties | | – | (324) |
| Currency translation differences | | (2) | (72) |
| New share capital issued | | 176 | 7 |
| Eurobond, debenture and share issue expenses | | – | (7) |
| Scrip dividends | | 4 | 56 |
| Goodwill arising on the acquisition of businesses | 25 | (89) | (3) |
| **Net increase (decrease) in shareholders' funds** | | **109** | **(331)** |
| Opening shareholders' funds | | 2,266 | 2,637 |
| Prior year adjustment | 18 | – | (40) |
| **Closing shareholders' funds** | | **2,375** | **2,266** |

g

## Hotel chain's P & L account and notes

The overall content of the P & L account of a plc or any company whose accounts are filed at Companies House is the same as for the small company's P & L account shown on page 53 above. However, there will possibly be more sub-headings and consequently detail which may be included as notes to the accounts.

As there is limited space in which to explain detail in the published accounts of a company, there is a limit to what can be gleaned from them. However, they are an essential element in understanding the sales and results of a business and can also indicate matters such as performance - where there are comparatives.

**A brief commentary on the hotel chain P & L account and relevant notes is as follows:**

Firstly, as was stated in Section 1 the P & L account should relate to the business. Generally published P & L accounts do not reveal much about the business. In spite of convention as to what cost of sales would be for most businesses the cost of sales in published accounts often includes overheads and other administration costs - the idea is to hide or obscure what gross profits or margins are being made. Notes to the accounts often contain more detail and analysis of costs. In the case of the hotel chain, note 3 gives an analysis of costs and this could be used to benchmark against other similar businesses. Also note 4 gives details of employee costs and numbers and again this could be used for bench marking purposes.

On the face of the P & L account there are figures covering continuing and discontinued operations and acquisitions, also for 2xx4 there is detail of restated figures. All of this is required by UK FRS 3 Reporting Financial Performance. Whilst this information may well be important it does seem unfortunate that it has to be disclosed on the face of the P & L account as it really does make interpretation more difficult.

The operating profit in 2xx5 of 248m is reasonable in relation to turnover of 1,753m. However, the relatively high gearing (borrowings are high) means that there are high interest charges and after tax and minority interests (amounts of profits in subsidiaries not wholly owned by the hotel chain and therefore attributable to outsiders - minorities) have been deducted, the remaining profit available for shareholders is only 89.

Of the profit available to shareholders of 89m, 69m is paid out as dividend and only 20m retained. Are they trying to keep shareholders happy? At least in the short-term.

**The Statement of Recognised Gains and Losses** is again required by FRS 3 and where a company has considerable revaluation amounts, currency gains or losses etc this may reveal useful information. For many companies it has little of interest in it - the companies' profits in the P & L account are the only profits.

**Reconciliation of Movements in Shareholders' Funds** is again required by FRS 3 and reconciles opening and closing shareholders funds. In the hotel chain's case there are many fairly clearly labelled movements. For most companies the movement is simply the retained profit for the year.

## US revenue or income statement (P & L account) structure and contents

The first point to note with a US revenue statement is that it is very similar to the UK P & L account, that is, it discloses income and costs giving income before and after taxes. Expenses are just listed, with no intervening calculation of gross or operating profit. Companies may disclose more detailed analysis of costs than in the UK.

eg

**Overleaf is an example: the oil corporation's consolidated statement of income.**

## The oil corporation – consolidated statement of income

| | 2xx5 | 2xx4 | 2xx3 |
|---|---|---|---|
| | | *(millions of dollars)* | |
| **Revenue** | | | |
| Sales and other revenue, including excise taxes | $121,804 | $112,128 | $109,532 |
| Earnings from equity interests and other revenue | 2,116 | 1,776 | 1,679 |
| Total revenue | $123,920 | $113,904 | $111,211 |
| **Costs and other deductions** | | | |
| Crude oil and product purchases | $49,695 | $46,430 | $46,124 |
| Operating expenses | 11,964 | 12,128 | 12,111 |
| Selling, general and administrative expenses | 7,629 | 7,226 | 7,009 |
| Depreciation and depletion | 5,386 | 5,015 | 4,884 |
| Exploration expenses, including dry holes | 693 | 666 | 648 |
| Interest expense | 571 | 773 | 681 |
| Excise taxes | 13,911 | 12,445 | 11,707 |
| Other taxes and duties. Other taxes and duties | 23,328 | 21,184 | 19,745 |
| Income applicable to minority and preferred interests | 301 | 233 | 250 |
| Total costs and other deductions | $113,478 | $106,100 | $103,159 |
| **Income before income taxes** | $10,442 | $7,804 | $8,052 |
| Income taxes | 3,972 | 2,704 | 2,772 |
| **Net income** | $6,470 | $5,100 | $5,280 |
| Net income per common share (dollars) | $5.18 | $4.07 | $4.21 |

## Consolidated statement of shareholders' equity

| | 2xx5 | | 2xx4 | | 2xx3 | |
|---|---|---|---|---|---|---|
| | Shares | Dollars | Shares | Dollars | Shares | Dollars |
| | | | *(millions of dollars)* | | | |
| Preferred stock outstanding at end of year | **7** | $454 | **9** | $554 | **11** | $668 |
| Guaranteed LESOP obligation | | (501) | | (613) | | (716) |
| Common stock issued at end of year | 1,813 | 2,822 | 1,813 | 2,822 | 1,813 | 2,822 |
| Earnings reinvested | | | | | | |
| At beginning of year | | $50,821 | | $49,365 | | $47,697 |
| Net income for year | | 6,470 | | 5,100 | | 5,280 |
| Dividends – common and preferred shares | | (3,752) | | (3,644) | | (3,612) |
| At end of year | | $53,539 | | $50,821 | | $49,365 |
| Cumulative foreign exchange translation adjustment | | | | | | |
| At beginning of year | | $848 | | $(370) | | $192 |
| Change during the year | | 491 | | 1,218 | | (562) |
| At end of year | | $1,339 | | $848 | | $(370) |
| Common stock held in treasury | | | | | | |
| At beginning of year | (571) | $(17,017) | (571) | $(16,977) | (571) | $(16,887) |
| Acquisitions, at cost | (9) | (628) | (4) | (220) | (5) | (323) |
| Dispositions | 9 | 428 | 4 | 180 | 5 | 233 |
| At end of year | (571) | $(17,217) | (571) | $(17,017) | (571) | $(16,977) |
| **Shareholders' equity at end of year** | | $40,436 | | $37,415 | | $34,792 |
| Common shares outstanding at end of year | 1,242 | | 1,242 | | 1,242 | |

## Comments on the corporation's consolidated statement of income

A brief commentary on the corporation's consolidated income statement and relevant notes is as follows.

Firstly, as was stated in Section 1, the income statement should relate to the business. In other words the reader should have some knowledge of the business, at least its areas of operation. The corporation is one of the oil majors, owning mineral rights and is an oil exploration and processing company.

As with earlier examples, the relevant amounts under each income statement heading should relate to the business activities carried out.

There are two sources of revenue, the principal one being from the corporation's businesses. The figure is shown including excise taxes which are shown separately as a cost. The actual income of the group of companies making up the corporation might more correctly be stated as $107,893 - the sales or revenue of the group.

The second source of revenue is the earnings from investments and any other miscellaneous sources.

Costs are listed under fairly clear headings. Although total figures for the group of companies of which the corporation is made up there is sufficient information to do some very basic bench marking. Detailed analysis could only be carried out with a further breakdown of the figures and details of the bases on which the figures were prepared.

Net income per common share is similar to earnings per share - see Chapter 6 Section 2.

## Interpretation of profit and loss accounts

To recap on the introductory points on interpretation of any financial statements:

**The financial statement should reflect the activities and position of the business being accounted for and reviewed.**

**With your knowledge of the business, look for obvious, significant types of income/expenses and their respective amounts in the profit and loss account.**

**The following illustration using the telecommunication company's P & L account is an example of what is meant by the above guidance:**

## Group profit and loss account
*For the year ended 31 March 2xx7*

| | Notes | 2xx7 £ million | 2xx6 £ million |
|---|---|---|---|
| **Turnover** | 1 | **14,935** | 14.446 |
| Operating costs (a) | 2 | **(11,690)** | (11,346) |
| Operating profit | | **3,245** | 3,100 |
| Group's share of profits of associated undertakings | | **139** | 82 |
| Profit on sale of group undertakings | 3 | **8** | 7 |
| Interest receivable | 4 | **206** | 201 |
| Interest payable | 4 | **(335)** | (371) |
| Premium on repurchase of bonds | 4 | **(60)** | – |
| **Profit on ordinary activities before taxation** | | **3,203** | 3,019 |
| Tax on profit on ordinary activities | 5 | **(1,102)** | (1,027) |
| **Profit on ordinary activities after taxation** | | **2,101** | 1,992 |
| Minority Interests | | **(24)** | (6) |
| Profit for the financial year | | **2,077** | 1,986 |
| Dividends: | 6 | | |
| Ordinary | | **(1,266)** | (1,184) |
| Special | | **(2,244)** | – |
| | | **(3,510)** | (1,184) |
| **Retained profit (transfer from reserves) for the financial year** | 19 | **(1,433)** | 802 |
| **Earnings per share** | 7 | **32.8p** | 31.6p |
| (a) including redundancy charges | | **367** | 421 |

## Group statement of total recognised gains and losses
*For the year ended 31 March*

| | 2xx7 £ million | 2xx6 £ million |
|---|---|---|
| Profit for the financial year | **2,077** | 1,986 |
| Currency movements arising on consolidation of foreign subsidiary and associated undertakings | **(76)** | 42 |
| Total recognised gains and losses | **2,001** | 2,028 |

## Notes to the financial statements

| | 2xx7 | 2xx6 |
|---|---|---|
| | £ million | £ million |
| **1. Turnover** | | |
| Inland telephone calls | **4,874** | 4,882 |
| International telephone calls | **1,809** | 1,980 |
| Telephone exchange line rentals | **2,811** | 2,685 |
| Private circuits | **1,124** | 1,056 |
| Mobile communications | **949** | 856 |
| Customer premises equipment supply | **914** | 946 |
| Yellow Pages and other directories | **438** | 408 |
| Other sales and services | **2,016** | 1,633 |
| Total turnover | **14,935** | 14,446 |

Turnover included income from telecommunication operators of £1,165m (2xx6 – £1,166m). In the year 3% (2xx6 – 2%) of turnover arose from operations outside the United Kingdom. There are no discontinued operations or acquisitions which require disclosure under Financial Reporting Standard 3.

| | 2xx7 | 2xx6 |
|---|---|---|
| | £ million | £ million |
| **2. Operating costs** | | |
| Staff costs: | | |
| Wages and salaries | **3,161** | 3,105 |
| Social security costs | **262** | 261 |
| Pension costs (***note 22***) | **291** | 284 |
| Employee share ownership scheme (a) | **64** | 30 |
| Total staff costs | **3,778** | 3,680 |
| Own work capitalised | **(399)** | (417) |
| Depreciation (note 11) | **2,265** | 2,189 |
| Payments to telecommunication operators | **1,476** | 1,383 |
| Redundancy charges (b) | **367** | 421 |
| Other operating costs | **4,309** | 4,193 |
| Other operating income | **(106)** | (103) |
| Total operating costs | **11,690** | 11,346 |
| Operating costs included the following: | | |
| Research and development | **291** | 282 |
| Rental costs relating to operating leases, including plant and equipment hire £10m (2xx6 – £23m) | **215** | 250 |

## Commentary on the telecommunication company's group profit and loss account

Group turnover is 14,935m, marginally up on the 14,446m the previous year. Details of costs are given in note 2 and these are separately commented upon below.

Operating profit of 3,245m is up on the 2xx6 figure of 3,100m and is 21.7 % of sales – this may appear quite high but a utility will have high infrastructure costs to be financed (high interest charges) and turnover to capital employed will be lower than many companies due again to the very high capital employed. (See Chapter 6 Sections 1 and 2 for further explanations and examples.)

The Group's share of profits of associated undertakings of 139m is the net income from investments which, whilst substantial shareholdings, will not be controlling investments (normally over 50% of voting power). Where there are controlling shareholdings, the turnover and profit will be included in full in the group figures above. Any small outside interests in controlled subsidiaries is later deducted as a one-off 'Cost' being minority interest, in this case 24m.

As with any developing group, there will be additions and disposals of subsidiaries and in this and the previous years there were small profits of 8m and 7m respectively.

The Companies Act requires disclosure of interest receivable and payable. Large and even small companies often have both interest income and expenses and it is common to show the detail in a note to the accounts. In the case of the telecommunication company, both figures are significant. They have accumulated a 'pile' of cash and short-term investments. At this time they were going to pay out a large special dividend, returning this cash to the shareholders. As would be expected of a utility, there are considerable borrowings and these give rise to the significant interest payable.

Premium on repurchase of bonds is a cost of redeeming bonds - borrowings. Companies often do this to reduce one type of borrowing - even at a premium - as they can arrange borrowing which has a lower effective interest rate. It may also be done to reduce borrowing to change the gearing of the company.

Details of the tax charge and the basis of the rate are given in the notes to the accounts.

After deducting taxation and minority interests there is the profit for the financial year - the profit available for shareholders, either to be paid out as dividend or retained and reinvested in the business's activities.

Dividends payments distinguish between ordinary, which would normally be a reasonable proportion of profit and tend to be fairy consistent year to year - that is, hopefully increasing as profits increase - and special dividends. The telecommunication company proposed a special dividend this year as they had accumulated substantial profits and related cash. It is often considered better to give cash back to shareholders by means of higher (or special dividends) rather than the company hang on to the cash and maybe invest it unwisely.

Normally a company would expect to transfer the balance of the undistributed profit to reserves (retained profit and loss account profit balance). Because of the payment of the special divided this year, there is a transfer out of previously accumulated reserves.

Earnings per share is often considered a very important measure of a company's performance. It is calculated by dividing the profit for the financial year available to shareholders by the number of shares in issue (see Chapter 6 Section 2 for more details). Again it is normally expected that a successful company will have a growing earnings per share (EPS) figure - as profits are meant to grow!

a) Including redundancy costs is additional information and could be shown in the notes. In this case, the restructuring of the company and the ensuing redundancies are a material figure and presumably the company wishes to get over the point that without this once-off (?) cost, the profit would have been higher.

## Group statement of recognised gains and losses

For the telecommunication company (as for many companies), this is a very simple statement in that recognised (realised) gains and losses – profit is only slightly lower than the reported profit for the financial year, the difference being a relatively small loss on currency movements.

## Checklist

✓ Profit and loss account income and cost profiles should reflect the nature of the business's activities.

# chapter three

section one

## Cash flow statements

## If there are profits there must be cash

If a business consistently generates profits from trading then there must be cash flowing into the business. However, this does not mean that the business will necessarily end up with a cash mountain - it depends on how cash generated is consumed or spent.

Cash could be spent on stocks or to fund debtors (sales to customers on credit) - cash could be tied up in working capital. Cash could be invested in tangible fixed assets. Cash could be distributed to the owners as dividends.

It is seldom the case that the profit for a year equals the cash balance available at the end of the year. For businesses both large and small it is generally considered wrong to have cash mountains, either the cash should be invested in fixed assets and working capital to make the business grow or returned to the owners for them to invest elsewhere.

If a business makes a loss it does not necessarily follow that in the short-term there will be no cash. However, if a business continues to make losses over a number of years then unless there is a constant investment of funds into the business there will be an increasing cash deficit and ultimately the company will become insolvent.

## Cash flow statements

Although it is not mandatory to include cash flow statements in small company accounts, cash flow statements have to be produced for larger companies and these are studied in Section 2 of this chapter.

Whilst not always required in published accounts cash flow statements may be required by banks or other investors in a company. They are a very useful aid to understanding a businesses performance and some might say give a clearer picture of financial performance and position of a business in that they are not obscured by accounting conventions such as accruals or depreciation - a clear cash flow picture is shown.

e.g.

## Cash flow statements – simple illustration

The profit and loss account for a small trader for the year ended 31 December 2xx7 shows that the business has made a profit of £3,000. It might be expected that as this is a very simple and straightforward business there will be a cash or bank balance of £3,000. Note that the word cash is very often used in businesses small and large when in fact the money will be in one or more bank accounts.

*Profit and loss account for the year ended 31 Dec 2xx7*

| | |
|---|---|
| Sales | 30,000 |
| Expenses | (25,000) |
| Depreciation | (2,000) |
| **Profit** | 3,000 |

However not all business transactions are for cash, that is paid or received as cash immediately. In this illustration £6,000 of sales have been made to a customer on credit, that is goods have been supplied but the customer does not have to pay cash for them until next year. Similarly £1,500 of expenses do not have to be paid for until next year. The £2,000 charge for depreciation is a cost of using the van or in respect of the loss of value of the van (see Chapter 4 Section 1), but there is no cash payment in respect of this cost. The cash flow in respect of the van occurs when it is purchased.

From the above it will be evident that not all the cash transactions which a business undertakes relate to purchasing or selling goods or services or paying for expenses - not all cash movements are related to P & L movements. Many cash transactions will be in respect of purchasing or selling assets or incurring or settling liabilities - they will be related to movements or changes in balance sheet items.

In this simple illustration the business has also taken out an £9,000 loan during the year and spent £8,000 on the purchase of a van.

*Cash flow statement for the year ended 31 Dec 2xx7*

| | | |
|---|---|---|
| Inflows | loan | 9,000 |
| | from sales | 24,000 |
| Outflows | expenses paid | (23,500) |
| | purchase of van | (8,000) |
| | **net cash flow inflow** | 1,500 |

The net effect of the differences between occurrence of P & L transactions and the receipt or payment of cash plus the other balance sheet movements in cash is that in this simple illustration the business has a closing cash balance of £1,500 rather than £3,000 which is the profit figure.The principal reason is of course the £6,000 outstanding from customers.

Cash flow statements do not require additional record keeping.They may be produced by identifying the movements between the beginning and ending balance sheets,(adjusting for non cash movements) or by appropriately summarising and classifying cash book entries.

An illustration of the preparation of a cash flow statement is set out opposite. Firstly we require the balance sheet and profit and loss figures.

**Balance sheet as at 31 December**

| | | 2007 | | 2006 |
|---|---|---|---|---|
| **Tangible fixed assets note 1** | | 1,200 | | 600 |
| **Current assets** | | | | |
| Stock | 600 | | 450 | |
| Debtors | 500 | | 430 | |
| Bank/cash | 390 | | 300 | |
| | 1,490 | | 1,180 | |
| **Current liabilities** | | | | |
| Creditors | (690) | | (580) | |
| | (690) | | (580) | |
| **Net currrent assets** | | 800 | | 600 |
| **Total assets less current liabilities** | | 2,000 | | 1,200 |
| Called up share capital | | 100 | | 100 |
| Profit and loss account | | 1,900 | | 1,100 |
| | | 2,000 | | 1,200 |

| **note 1 - fixed asset detail** | Fixtures & fittings |
|---|---|
| **Cost** | |
| at 1 Jan 2007 | 1,000 |
| Additions | 800 |
| **at 31 Dec 2007** | **1,800** |
| **Accumulated depreciation** | |
| at 1 Jan 2007 | 400 |
| Charge for year | 200 |
| **at 31 Dec 2007** | **600** |
| **Net book amount** | |
| at 1 Jan 2006 | 600 |
| **at 31 Dec 2007** | **1,200** |

**Profit and loss account for the year**

| | | |
|---|---|---|
| Sales | | 8,000 |
| Cost of sales | | (5,000) |
| Gross profit | | 3,000 |
| admin costs | (2,000) | |
| depreciation | (200) | |
| | | (2,200) |
| Operating profit | | 800 |

A common method or producing a cash flow statement is to start with the accounting profit and adjust this for timing differences and non cash transactions or entries.That is start with the £800 profit, add back depreciation which does not involve the movement of cash and then adjust for increases or decreases in cash tied up in working capital items such as debtors, stock and creditors.This is the cash surplus or deficit arising from trading.The profit (or loss) is calculated taking account of relevant non cash transactions - see Chapter 4 Section 1.

The cash flow statement then shows cash spent or received in respect of fixed assets, changes in loans or equity capital.

**Cash flow statement**

| | | |
|---|---|---|
| Profit per P&L account | | 800 |
| add back depreciation - not a cash movement | | 200 |
| changes in working capital | | |
| | increase in stock | -150 |
| | increase in debtors | -70 |
| | increase in creditors | 110 |
| | | 890 |
| Purchase of fixed assets | | -800 |
| | net cash inflow/outflow (-) | **90** |
| | change in bank/cash | **90** |

If the cash book data was available it would also be possible to prepare the cash flow statement directly from the cash book.

**Cash summary for the year**

| | IN | OUT | |
|---|---|---|---|
| opening balance | 300 | | |
| from debtors | 7,930 | 5,040 | to creditors |
| | | 2,000 | on admin expenses |
| | | 800 | new fixed asset |
| | | 390 | closing balance |
| | 8,230 | 8,230 | |

In this illustration the net cash movement arising from P & L transactions is an £890 increase

| | |
|---|---|
| from debtors | 7,930 |
| to creditors | -5,040 |
| on admin expenses | -2,000 |
| 'cash' profit | 890 |

and a decrease from balance sheet movements - the £800 spent on fixed assets. The net effect is the increase in cash of £90.

## What can cash flow statements tell us?

A cash flow statement and the notes thereto will explain why the reported accounting profit is not the same amount as the net cash generated from trading. It will show other sources of funds and uses, for example from money invested in the business or borrowed by the business and where the money has been invested, eg in tangible fixed assets.

As discussed in the chapters on balance sheets and profit and loss accounts **cash flow statements should reflect the cash flows of the business as described**.

They are a useful means of understanding a businesses progress, profitability and disposition of assets and liabilities, particularly cash.

Section 2 contains the cash flow statement for the small business studied in Sections 1 of Chapters 1 and 2. This has more detail than the simple examples studied so far and is followed by an example of the formal layout required by the accounting standards (International Accounting Standard 7 or UK Financial Reporting Standard 1).

## Checklist

- ✓ An amount of profit does not mean there will be an equal amount of cash at the end of a period.
- ✓ Cash can be 'tied up' in working capital – stock, debtors and creditors, yet another reason for managing – minimising working capital.
- ✓ Cash must be generated to allow investment and to give returns to investors.
- ✓ Cash flow statements should confirm the cash position of a business.
- ✓ Do you know your businesses cash flows?

# chapter three

section two

## Cash flow statements

Published cash flow statements

Definitions

Compiling and interpreting a cash flow statement

Checklist

## Published cash flow statements

The objectives of a published cash flow statement as set out in Financial Reporting Standard (FRS) 1 are to ensure that the reporting entity:

- Reports its cash generation and cash absorption for a period by highlighting the significant components of cash flow in a way which facilitates comparison of the cash flow performance of different business types.
- Provides information which assists in the assessment of its liquidity, solvency and financial adaptability.

**Scope:** large and medium companies, but not subsidiaries (owned 90% or more) if consolidated cash flow statement is published. Also, not various specialised business types defined in paragraph 5 of the FRS and not small companies as defined by UK company legislation.

### What is required?

An entity which is required to produce a cash flow statement should classify its cash flows for the accounting period under the following standard headings:

**Operating activities (direct or indirect method)**

**Returns on investments and servicing of finance**

**Taxation**

**Capital expenditure and financial investment**

**Acquisitions and disposals**

**Equity dividends paid**

**Management of liquid resources**

**Financing**

Management of liquid resources and financing may be combined under a single heading provided subtotals are given for each.

The information given by a cash flow statement is best appreciated in the context of the information given in the balance sheet and P & L account. FRS1 requires two reconciliations, one between the operating profit and the net cash flow from operating activities and the other between the movement in cash in the period and the movement in net debt. Neither reconciliation forms part of the cash flow statement and each may be given in either a statement adjoining the cash flow statement or in a separate note.

Movement in net debt should identify its components below and reconcile these to the opening and closing balance sheet amounts.

*Cash flows of the entity*

The acquisition or disposal of subsidiary undertakings (excluding cash balances)

*Other non cash changes*

The recognition of changes in market value and exchange rate movements.

### Operating activities (direct or indirect method*)

Cash flows from operating activities are in general the cash effects of transactions and other events relating to operating or trading activities, normally shown in the profit and loss account in arriving at operating profit.

A reconciliation between the reported operating profit in the P & L account and the net cash flow from operating activities should be given. This reconciliation (which is essential when trying to understand the cash flows) is not part of the cash flow statement! It should be kept separate.

The reconciliation is one which aims to 'dis-' or 'un-' accrue the operating profit, that is profit will be adjusted for movements in stocks, debtors, creditors and depreciation and other non cash charges.

***Direct or indirect:** Operating cash flows may be presented using the direct method - the gross receipts and payments which net to the operating profit, or the indirect method which starts with the reported operating profit. In either case the operating profit is reconciled back to cash flow rather than accounting profit.

## Returns on investments and servicing of finance

Returns on investments and servicing of finance include receipts from the ownership of investments (interest received and dividends received) and payments to providers of finance, non-equity shareholders, etc.

With the majority of companies the net total under this heading is an outflow - payments to providers of finance - the standard wording is misleading.

## Taxation

Taxation cash flows should be reported. As the tax payments may arise out of complex computations, particularly for a group, it is considered impractical to attempt to analyse the taxation cash flows in any great detail. Taxation cash flows arising from distinct capital and revenue profits should be disclosed in a separate section within the cash flow statement.

## Capital expenditure and financial investment

The cash flows included under this heading are those related to the acquisition or disposal of any fixed asset other than one required to be classified under 'acquisitions and disposals' below and any current asset investment not included as liquid resources.

## Acquisitions and disposals

These are cash flows related to the acquisition or disposal of any trade or business, or of an investment in an entity that is or, as a result of a transaction, becomes or ceases to be either an associate, a joint venture, or a subsidiary undertaking.

## Equity dividends paid

Cash outflows in respect of dividends paid on the reporting entity's equity shares, excluding advanced corporation tax.

## Management of liquid resources

These are cash flows in respect of liquid resources.The entity should explain what it includes as liquid resources and any changes in its policy.

## Financing

These cash flows comprise receipts or repayments of principal from or to external providers of finance.

The cash flows of the above two sections may be combined provided that separate sub-totals are given for each heading.

## Definitions

### Cash

Cash in hand and deposits repayable on demand with any qualifying financial institution, less overdrafts from any qualifying financial institution repayable on demand. Deposits are repayable on demand if they can be withdrawn at any time without notice and without penalty or if a maturity or period of notice of not more than 24 hours or one working day has been agreed. Cash includes cash in hand and deposits denominated in foreign currencies.

### Cash flow

An increase or decrease in an amount of cash.

### Liquid resources

Current asset investments held as readily disposable stores of value. A readily disposable investment is one which:

- is disposable by the reporting entity without curtailing or disrupting its business;

*and is either*

- readily convertible into known amounts of cash at or close to its carrying amount, or
- traded in an active market.

### Net debt

The borrowings of the reporting entity (comprising debt together with related derivatives, and obligations under finance leases) less cash and liquid resources. Where cash and liquid resources exceed the borrowings of the entity, reference should be made to '**net funds**' rather than to net debt.

### Overdraft

A borrowing facility repayable on demand which is used by drawing on a current account with a qualifying institution.

### Equity dividends

Dividends relating to equity shares.These are defined most helpfully(!) in UK FRS 4 Capital Instruments as 'shares other than non-equity shares'.An example of non-equity shares is preference shares which are entitled to a fixed dividend payable before ordinary (equity) share dividends.

## Compiling and interpreting a cash flow statement

The example overleaf is based on the simple businesses balance sheet and P & L account studied in Chapters 1 and 2. To compile a cash flow statement it is necessary to have the previous year's or period's balance sheet.

**Balance sheet as at 31 December**

| | | 2006 | | 2005 |
|---|---|---|---|---|
| **Tangible fixed assets note 1** | | 74,800 | | 53,400 |
| **Current assets** | | | | |
| Stock | 22,500 | | 14,600 | |
| Debtors | 31,600 | | 15,400 | |
| Cash | 2,200 | | 1,300 | |
| | 56,300 | | 31,300 | |
| **Current liabilities** | | | | |
| Overdraft | (13,900) | | (1,900) | |
| Trade creditors | (23,600) | | (19,800) | |
| Taxation | (8,700) | | (1,700) | |
| | (46,200) | | (23,400) | |
| **Net currrent assets** | | 10,100 | | 7,900 |
| **Total assets less current liabilities** | | 84,900 | | 61,300 |
| **Creditors: amounts falling due after more than one year** | | | | |
| Bank loan | | (15,000) | | (10,000) |
| | | 69,900 | | 51,300 |
| Called up share capital | | 20,000 | | 20,000 |
| Profit and loss account | | 49,900 | | 31,300 |
| | | 69,900 | | 51,300 |

**note 1**

| **Cost** | Land and buildings | Fixtures and fittings | Motor vehicles | Totals |
|---|---|---|---|---|
| at 1 Jan 2006 | 51,100 | 5,500 | 0 | 56,600 |
| Additions | 0 | 16,000 | 9,200 | 25,200 |
| **at 31 Dec 2006** | **51,100** | **21,500** | **9,200** | **81,800** |
| **Accumulated depreciation** | | | | |
| at 1 Jan 2006 | 0 | 3,200 | 0 | 3,200 |
| Charge for year | 0 | 1,500 | 2,300 | 3,800 |
| **at 31 Dec 2006** | **0** | **4,700** | **2,300** | **7,000** |
| **Net book amount** | | | | |
| at 1 Jan 2006 | 51,100 | 2,300 | 0 | 53,400 |
| **at 31 Dec 2006** | **51,100** | **16,800** | **6,900** | **74,800** |

**Profit and loss account for the year ended**

| | | 2xx6 | | 2xx5 |
|---|---|---|---|---|
| Sales | | 201,000 | | 198,000 |
| Cost of sales | | (105,100) | | (102,400) |
| Gross profit | | 95,900 | | 95,600 |
| Admin costs | (62,600) | | (58,700) | |
| Depreciation | (3,800) | | (1,600) | |
| | | (66,400) | | (60,300) |
| Operating profit | | 29,500 | | 35,300 |
| Interest charge | | (1,400) | | (1,150) |
| Profit before tax | | 28,100 | | 34,150 |
| Taxation | | (7,500) | | (9,200) |
| Profit available for shareholders | | 20,600 | | 24,950 |
| Dividend paid | | (2,000) | | (18,000) |
| Profit retained | | 18,600 | | 6,950 |

As a basis for understanding and preparing the formal cash flow statement, it may be sensible to simply analyse the sources and applications or uses of cash during the year. Most of the figures come from the movement in the balance sheet figures between the beginning and end of the year. Adjustments have to be made for items which do not involve the movement of funds or cash. For example, depreciation has to be added back to profit to give the cash 'profit'.

**Sources and uses of funds**

| | sources | uses |
|---|---|---|
| profit | 29,500 | |
| depreciation | 3,800 | |
| loans | 5,000 | |
| stocks | | 7,900 |
| debtors | | 16,200 |
| creditors | 3,800 | |
| taxation (paid) | | 500 |
| purchase of fixed assets | | 25,200 |
| interest paid | | 1,400 |
| dividend paid | | 2,000 |
| | 42,100 | 53,200 |
| **net application** | **-11,100** | |
| **change in cash and bank** | | |
| decrease in cash | 900 | |
| increase in overdraft | -12,000 | |
| | **-11,100** | |

This indicates that whilst the company is profitable, there is a heavy use of funds, both in fixed asset investment and invested (or tied up?) in working capital items, in particular stock and debtors.

The above figures may then be analysed under the appropriate heading in the published cash flow statement.

As is almost inevitable with any example, it is clear that the accounting profit will not be the same as the cash surplus or deficit for the year. There is the need for a statement or note to reconcile the profit per accounts with the cash flow generated or used by activities.

From the above figures note 2 reconciling accounting profit to cash flow from operating activities may be prepared.

**note 2 cash flow from operating activities**

| | | |
|---|---|---|
| Profit per accounts | | 29,500 |
| add back depreciation | | 3,800 |
| changes in working capital | | |
| | stock | -7,900 |
| | debtors | -16,200 |
| | creditors | 3,800 |
| cash flow from operating activities | | 13,000 |

In this case the distinction between profit and cash is very clear - operating profit is 29,000 but net cash flow from trading operations is only 13,000 - the principal reasons are the increases in stocks and debtors.This statement or note is not part of the formal Cash Flow Statement as required by FRS 1 or International Accounting Standard (IAS 7) - to the author this seems very odd, as it is most often the changes in the elements of working capital which are most significant.

Once cash flow from operating activities has been identified the cash flows can be analysed under their appropriate headings.

**Cash flow statement for the year ended 31 December 2006**

| | | | |
|---|---|---|---|
| **cash flow from operating activities** | | **13,000** | **note 2** |
| **paid to providers of finance** | *returns on investments and servicing of finance* | | |
| | interest paid | -1,400 | |
| **taxation** | tax paid | -500 | |
| charge +/- change in tax creditor | | | |
| | | **11,100** | |
| **investments** | *capital expenditure and financial investment* | | |
| | purchase of fixed assets | -25,200 | |
| | acquisitions and disposal | | |
| **equity dividends paid** | | | |
| | dividends paid | -2,000 | |
| | | **-16,100** | |
| **management of liquid resources** | | | |
| | change in cash | -900 | |
| | change in overdraft | 12,000 | |
| | | **-5,000** | |
| **financing** | | | |
| | increase in long-term loan | **-5,000** | |

In this simple example the management of liquid resources and financing have not been combined as, in the author's view it is important to clearly distinguish between short and long-term financing. Also it is considered helpful to see how the overall cash flows of a business are managed and how the cash flow requirements are funded.

Many published cash flow statements often have very confusing layouts with respect to management of liquid resources and financing.

Understanding where the figures come from and the definitions of the headings used in a cash flow statement is the basis for interpreting them.

In the above example the following are the important issues:

- Cash flow from operating activities - cash (the operating surplus) is considerably less than accounting profit due to money tied up in working capital items, particularly stock and debtors.
- However, the company does have positive cash flow from operating after paying interest and tax.
- Cash spent on new fixed asset investment is considerably in excess of internally generated funds.
- The cash invested (or tied up) in working capital and fixed assets has been funded from operating activities, by increasing overdraft and long-term finance.

It would be important to check that the increase in overdraft was intentional or planned and related to the increase in stock and debtors. Also it would be important to check that the increase in overdraft and related working capital items was planned as being temporary.

## Interpreting cash flow statements

g

The following page sets out the cash flow statement with relevant notes of the hotel chain for the year ended 31 January 2xx5. (The related balance sheet and profit and loss account can be found on pages 31 and 66.)

Note 21 illustrates how the accounting profit is reconciled back to net inflow from operating activities. As might be expected from a business with considerable tangible fixed assets but fairly low level of working capital the major adjustment is in respect of depreciation added back as the depreciation charge does not involve the movement of funds.

As with any interpretation of figures it is important not to get bogged down in detail and the comments which follow the cash flow statement are in respect of the material figures under each heading.

## Consolidated cash flow statement

*For the year ended 31 January 2xx5*

| | Notes | 2xx5 £ million | Restated 2xx4 £ million |
|---|---|---|---|
| **Net cash inflow from operating activities** | 21 | **341** | **309** |
| **Returns on investments and servicing of finance** | | | |
| Interest paid | | (104) | (112) |
| Finance charges paid under sale and leaseback agreements | | (34) | (33) |
| Interest received | | 2 | 5 |
| Dividends paid to shareholders | | (61) | (5) |
| Dividends paid to minority interests | | (8) | (13) |
| Net cash outflow from returns on investments and servicing of finance | | (205) | (158) |
| Taxation paid | | (13) | (2) |
| **Net cash inflow before investing activities** | | **123** | **149** |
| **Investing activities** | | | |
| Purchase of tangible fixed assets | | (147) | (144) |
| Disposal of fixed assets | | 54 | 33 |
| Sale of subsidiaries | 24 | 150 | 38 |
| Acquisition of businesses | 25 | (204) | (19) |
| Cash and cash equivalents of businesses acquired | 25 | 37 | – |
| **Net cash outflow from investing activities** | | **(110)** | **(92)** |
| **Net cash inflow before financing** | | **13** | **57** |
| **Financing** | | | |
| Issue of ordinary share capital | | 176 | 7 |
| Eurobond, debenture and share issue expenses | | – | (7) |
| Capital market issues | | 100 | 540 |
| Capital market redemptions | | (140) | – |
| Net repayment of bank loans | | (95) | (194) |
| **Net cash inflow from equity, bank and other borrowings** | 22 | **41** | **346** |
| Other financing | | – | 4 |
| **Net cash inflow from financing** | | **41** | **350** |
| Increase in cash and cash equivalents | 23 | (54) | (407) |
| **Financing of net cash inflow** | | **(13)** | **(57)** |

| | Notes | 2xx5 | Restated 2xx4 |
|---|---|---|---|
| | | £ million | £ million |
| **Analysis of operating free cash flow (before dividends)** | | | |
| Profit before tax | | 127 | 77 |
| Depreciation/non-cash items | | 87 | 97 |
| Working capital – operating | | (4) | (13) |
| – interest | | (5) | 8 |
| Taxation paid | | (13) | (2) |
| Purchase of tangible fixed assets | | (147) | (144) |
| Disposal of fixed assets | | 54 | 33 |
| **Operating free cash flow (before dividends)** | | **99** | **56** |

| **21 Reconciliation of operating profit to net cash inflow from operating activities** | 2xx5 | 2xx4 |
|---|---|---|
| | £ million | £ million |
| Operating profit | 258 | 225 |
| Depreciation | 88 | 97 |
| Other non-cash movements | (1) | – |
| Net increase in working capital | (4) | (13) |
| **Net cash inflow from operating activities** | **341** | **309** |

| **22 Analysis of changes in financing during the year** | Share capital (including premium) £ million | Bank and other borrowings £ million | Total financing £ million |
|---|---|---|---|
| Balance at 31 January 2xx4 | **336** | **1,149** | **1,485** |
| Prior year adjustment | – | 465 | 465 |
| Balance at 31 January 2xx4 restated | **336** | **1,614** | **1,950** |
| Issues of ordinary share capital | 176 | – | 176 |
| Capital market issues | – | 100 | 100 |
| Capital market redemptions | – | (140) | (140) |
| Net repayment of bank loans | – | (95) | (95) |
| **Cash inflow (outflow) from financing** | **176** | **(135)** | **41** |
| Increase in finance lease obligations | – | 10 | 10 |
| Loans of subsidiary undertakings acquired during the year | – | 92 | 92 |
| **Balance at 31 January 2xx5** | **512** | **1,581** | **2,093** |

Net cash flow from operating is a positive 341m.

205m is used to satisfy the providers of finance - this seems very high in relation to cash flow generated from operating. This infers that profits and thus cash flow are poor and or borrowings are high.

13m is paid in tax - this may be good, but it does indicate a lack of profitability.

There is still a positive cash flow of 123m before any investment.

There is 147m spent on tangible fixed assets and 205m spent on business acquisition.This has been partly financed by the sale of subsidiary businesses.

The net effect is that nearly all of the free cash flow remaining from operating activities has been used for expansion and hopefully profitable growth.

There remains an overall net cash inflow of 13m.

There have been considerable changes in sources of finance, particularly loans have been repaid from the 176m proceeds of new ordinary shares issued.There has also been considerable change in loans - the capital market redemptions and issues.

The net effect on cash and cash equivalents is an increase of 54m.

In summary, cash has obviously been managed, but there is considerable activity. Questions which might have been asked are:

- Is the business generating sufficient cash flow?
- Are borrowings too high?
- Why buy and sell businesses?
- Why raise money from shareholders? Will they get an adequate return on their new investment?

## Checklist

- ✓ Does the cash flow statement agree with the 'story'?
- ✓ Does the cash flow appear to be managed?

# Accounting records and systems

Why have accounting records?

Distinction between accounting systems and accounting records

Checklist

## Why have accounting records?

The reasons for maintaining accounting records of a business are many.

The prime reason is to know how the business is performing and to keep track of assets and liabilities. For many smaller businesses the owners keep track of their businesses by being aware of their bank and cash transactions.

Another reason for maintaining accounting records is because they are required by various authorities.

> UK company law requires proper accounting records to be maintained for incorporated companies.
>
> The Inland Revenue or equivalent authorities in other countries require adequate records of income, expenses, assets etc so that income, corporation or capital taxes can be correctly levied.
>
> Customs & Excise or equivalent sales tax and duty authorities require appropriate records relating to selling or purchasing, importing or exporting of goods and services as a base for calculating VAT, sales taxes, duties etc.
>
> Listed companies - companies whose shares are listed on a recognised stock exchange are required to produce regular - often quarterly statements of profit or loss, asset and cash positions.
>
> There may also be other agencies such as statistical collection authorities who demand regular returns which again require businesses to maintain proper accounting records.

It is very important that business people and even more so regulatory authorities don't forget that the prime reason for maintaining accounting records is to assist the owners/ managers to run and control a successful business.

## Distinction between accounting systems and accounting records

### Accounting systems

An accounting system would normally be considered as meaning the entire process by which final financial and management accounts are produced. The use of 'final' is meant to imply, complete and correct, year or period end accounts.

For a very small business there will be a very limited system. As illustration, for a small retailer, there may be till rolls which are summarised on weekly sales sheets; there will be a record of goods ordered and deliveries received. A cash book of bankings linked to sales summary figures and an analysis of cheques paid for purchases, wages and overhead expenses. The owners/managers could produce weekly summaries from this data to assist in running and controlling the business. The records listed above would then typically be passed to the businesses external accountants for them to produce the final, annual accounts required for the purposes listed above.

For a large group of companies there will be systems within each company or division with obviously much more complete and regular recording and assembling of figures into weekly and certainly monthly full management accounts - detailed P & L accounts and a balance sheet.

Accounting systems and controls (internal controls) are considered further in Section 2.

## Accounting records

The UK Companies Act requires the following in respect of accounting records:

1) Every company shall cause accounting records to be kept in accordance with this section.

2) The accounting records shall be sufficient to show and explain the company's transactions, and shall be such as to:

   a) Disclose with reasonable accuracy, at any time, the financial position of the company at that time, and

   b) Enable the directors to ensure that any balance sheet and profit and loss account prepared under this part comply with the requirements of this Act as to the form and content of company accounts and otherwise.

3) The accounting records shall in particular contain:

   a) Entries from day to day of all money received and expended by the company, and the matters in respect of which the receipt and expenditure takes place, and

   b) A record of the assets and liabilities of the company.

4) If the company's business involves dealing in goods, the accounting records shall contain:

   a) Statements of stock held by the company at the end of each financial year of the company.

   b) All statements of stocktakings from which any such statement of stock as is mentioned in paragraph (a) above has been or is to be prepared, and

   c) Except in the case of goods sold by way of ordinary retail trade, statements of all goods sold and purchased, showing the goods and buyers and sellers in sufficient detail to enable all these to be identified.

In the above illustration the small company has piecemeal accounting records which are appropriate and adequate for its size and form the basis from which the required final annual statutory accounts can be produced. They also permit the production of such management figures as are considered necessary.

For a large company or group as the illustration suggests there would be complete and regular recording and assembling of figures and they would maintain what should correctly be called a general ledger, but which is more often called a nominal ledger. The data in the general ledger will come from and be further analysed in subsidiary ledgers.

An illustration of the typical structure for the accounting records of a trading company can be found in Section 2.

This section deals with how figures may be recorded by a method which aims to allow easy production of a P & L account and balance sheet when required - book keeping, strictly double entry book keeping.

Another aim of book keeping is to ensure that figures are complete and as free from error as possible. Book keeping cannot ensure this, but it does give a sound basis on which controls over completeness accuracy and validity of figures may be built.

Because of its fundamental aims to record as completely and accurately as possible the events (income and expenses), assets and liabilities of a business, book keeping may appear to 'make a meal' of recording figures - figures are recorded in two places when one entry would appear adequate. It is the control aspect of the exercise which requires this as much as anything.

Firstly definitions. The simplest way of defining what assets, liabilities, income and expenses are, is to consider examples of each. On page 104 in italics there are the definitions dreamt up by academic economists/accountants - they are not really very helpful.

### Assets

Assets are most often tangible real things - buildings, furniture, cash in hand or deposited at a bank or through a sales agreement debtors owe money.

Assets **owe** value **to** the business - they are thus called debtor (or debit) balances.

### Liabilities

Liabilities are amounts of money owed to suppliers of goods or services or to banks or other lenders. Amounts invested by shareholders - share capital can also be considered a liability as they, the shareholders are owed the money back, albeit they could only have the money returned if the company was wound up - liquidated with sufficient funds to repay them.

Liabilities are amounts **owed** to others **by** the business - they are called creditor (or credit) balances

### Income/sales/revenue

These are the amounts due from selling goods or services. It is the sum of events - the sales transactions for a period in money terms. The other side of the double entry equation is that for every sales transaction there should be an equal in amount, asset increase - either cash received or debtor recorded as due.

Income received or receivable by a business results in a credit balance.

## Expenses/costs/purchases/overheads

These are the amounts due to suppliers (employees can also be considered as suppliers - of labour) in respect of goods and services supplied. The other side of the double entry equation is that for every purchase transaction there should be an equal in amount, asset decrease (cash paid out) or liability increase - creditor recorded as payable.

Expenses are payable or **owed by** the business - they result in called debit balances.

There are thus only two signs in book keeping debit and credit or debtor and creditor may be more appropriate words for balance sheet items. There are the two statements - P & L account and balance sheets to be produced, therefore the following simple matrix may be considered:

| | **Balance sheet** | |
|---|---|---|
| | **Asset**<br>owes value to<br>the business | **Liability**<br>business owes<br>to outsiders |
| ***examples*** | motor car<br>stock | due to supplier<br>bank loan |
| ***book keeping term*** | debtor or<br>**debit balance** | creditor or<br>**credit balance** |
| | **P & L account** | |
| | **Expense**<br>amount due by the business<br>(hopefully for some value!) | **Income**<br>amount due to the business |
| ***examples*** | stationery<br>labour | sales<br>interest on bank deposit |
| ***book keeping term*** | **debit balance** | **credit balance** |

The words 'debit' and 'credit' may appear to be used in contradictory ways, but it important to appreciate the different nature of the P & L account and balance sheet. One way of considering them is to think of the P & L accounts recording events and the balance sheet as recording the position of the business - the assets and liabilities resulting form the events in which the business gets involved.

Book keeping is about recording every single event or transaction into which a business enters. A sale (presumably good news) gives rise to credits in the P & L account and a debit (debtor) increase in asset in the balance sheet, again good news.

An expense (not good news, but hopefully the incurring of expense is worthwhile or at least necessary) gives rise to debits in the P & L account and either a credit - increase in liabilities (creditors) in the balance sheet or a decrease in assets - in arithmetical terms this is a credit to the asset account thus of course decreasing the debtor balance!

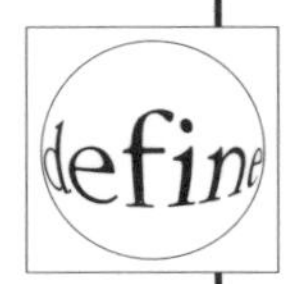


### The academic – 'accounting framework' definitions

***Assets:*** *probable future economic benefits obtained or controlled by a particular entity as a result of past transactions or events.*

***Liabilities:*** *probable future sacrifices of economic benefits arising from present obligations of a particular entity to transfer assets or provide services to other entities in the future as a result of past transactions or events.*

***Income:*** *is increases in economic benefits during the accounting period in the form of inflows or enhancements of assets or decrease of liabilities that result in increases in equity, other than those relating to contributions from equity participants. The definitions of* *income encompasses both revenue and gains, and revenue arises in the course of ordinary activities of an enterprise and is referred to by different names, such as sales, fees, interest, dividends, royalties and rent.*

***Expenses:*** *are decreases in economic benefits during an accounting period in the form of outflows or depletions of assets or incurrences of liabilities that result in decreases in equity, other than those relating to distributions to equity participants. Thus the characteristics of expenses include the following:*

1. *Sacrifices involved in carrying out the earnings process*
2. *Actual or expected cash outflows resulting from ordinary activities*
3. *Outflows reported gross.*

## Book keeping

The following example sets out how business transactions would be recorded under a system of double entry book keeping.

The required accounts are set up to record P & L and balance sheet transactions. Each account has columns for the debit (debtor) and credit (creditor) entries. Normally the accounts are kept in a logical order – in this case balance sheet accounts on the left and P & L accounts to the right.

The accounts can then record the events/transactions as they occur. For every debit there must be equal credit – the total of all debits must at all times equal the total of all credits.

**Balance sheet accounts** / **Profit and loss accounts**

**1**

**Cash**

| | Db | | Cr |
|---|---|---|---|
| **balance** | **350** | | |
| | | **stock** | **300** |

**Stock for sale - cost of sales**

| | Db | | Cr |
|---|---|---|---|
| **paid cash** | **300** | | |

**2**

**Cash**

| | Db | | Cr |
|---|---|---|---|
| balance | 350 | | |
| | | stock | 300 |
| **from** selling | **700** | | |

**Sales**

| | Db | | Cr |
|---|---|---|---|
| | | **cash received** | **700** |

**3**

**Capital**

| | Db | | Cr |
|---|---|---|---|
| | | original* | 350 |
| | | **profit retained** | **400** |

**The P & L account**

| | Db | | Cr |
|---|---|---|---|
| **Cost of Sales** | **300** | **Sales** | **700** |
| **added to capital** | **400** | **profit (credit) balance** | **400** |

* there must have been original capital of 350 to match the 350 cash balance brought forward

**Profit and loss account for the period ended _ _ _ _ _**

| | |
|---|---|
| **Sales** | **700** |
| **Cost of sales** | **300** |
| **Net profit** | **400** |

**Balance sheet as at _ _ _ _ _ _**

| | | |
|---|---|---|
| **Assets employed current assets** | | |
| **Cash** | **750** | original 350 less 300 plus 700 |
| **Financed by** | | |
| **Capital** | **750** | original 350 plus 400 profit retained |

1 A 350 cash balance, a debtor balance as cash owes value to the business. This is reduced by the purchase of stock.

   Stock for sale is a cost - a debit or expense.

2 Customers hand over cash for the stock received by them the business receives the asset cash - a debtor which owes value to the business.

   Sales are income - credits to the P & L account.

3 The P & L account is a summary account - the profit is the net of sales less all costs. In this case the balancing figure is very obviously 400 profit.

   The profit may either be paid out (dividend) or retained in the business as retained profit or capital reinvested.

It is the end results, the P & L account and balance sheet which are important to managers and if the process of getting there seems rather heavy handed or tedious do not worry - presumably you can leave the book keeping to the accountants or 'bean counters'. If you are very keen! or need to understand the subject in more detail then there are further examples of book keeping in Section 2.

### There is no such thing as 'just a figure'

The above examples show the operation of book keeping. You do not have to do this, but the point is, managers should be aware that transactions are recorded and the often heard quote 'don't worry it's just a figure' is not a very good answer to anyone enquiring about figures in a report. Many accountants seem to forget the tenets of double entry book keeping and the fact that they ought to be able to trace any figure back to source. Even in today's paperless businesses the operation of a book keeping and internal control systems (see Section 2) mean that figures ought to be traceable.

In recent frauds in banks and the financial sector it is the apparent surprise of directors and managers, that money has disappeared without their knowledge which is so unbelievable - there has to be at least one half of the accounting entry - or are the accounts full of 'just figures' - the whole thing is a fraud.

## Checklist

- ✓ There are reasons for keeping records.
- ✓ What are yours?
- ✓ You have to keep a minimum level of records.

# Accounting records and systems

## Accounting systems and procedures

Maintaining accounting records - book keeping - is at the heart of accounting as without adequate records there would be no financial statements. Further, without proper management and internal controls, record keeping would inevitably be prone to error and abuse (from carelessness, negligence or fraud).

Book keeping is at the heart of a business's accounting system and it is there as there is the need to manage the businesses assets/liabilities and income expense - rather than just to occupy some accountants time!

Accounting records are maintained for many reasons because:

- The law says so
- Tax authorities require records
- Managers have to manage (with the aid of accurate figures)
- Shareholders need to know what is going on
- Outsiders want to know how the business is progressing and its financial status.

All are valid reasons, but the prime one (accepting of course that you must comply with the relevant law) must be that it is necessary for the owners and thus managers to know the amount and proper classification of assets/liabilities and income/expenditure. Practice managers will need to know specific figures and may not be interested in the entire picture. For example, sales will be important to the sales team. Details of amounts, volumes, values and other non financial details (eg units of production) will be required. There may be much more than is required for financial accounting purposes.

Thus a company will have to have records and a means of managing the flow of documents which are required to manage the business. There will be a need for accounting procedures.

It is appropriate to distinguish accounting ledgers, systems and procedures and internal control.

**Accounting ledgers** are the sets of double entry records which contain the necessary information from which the annual statutory and intervening financial and management accounts can be prepared. The ledgers also contain all necessary records of transactions undertaken by the company. A classic structure of a set of ledgers is set out below.

**Accounting procedures** are procedures relating to the entry and recording of data. They are the instructions which set out how processing and record keeping is to be carried out.

**An accounting system** is the set of ledgers, procedures and controls which ensure that all necessary transactions are recorded completely, accurately and validly. Traditionally it was the accounting system which was seen as the essential centre for a company's data collection. Today often systems are centred on other areas – eg sales data and the accounting data is to a degree secondary. This may well be correct, but it should never be forgotten that reliable financial data is essential.

**A system of internal control** is the whole system of routines and controls, financial and wider which are considered necessary to ensure that assets and liabilities and income and expenditure of the business are reported faithfully.

## Classic ledger structure

The simplest form of a ledger containing all the necessary information from which accounts can be prepared is a fully detailed and analysed cash book for a small business. This contains only one side of the double entry, but should have all the necessary information from which a set of accounts can be prepared.

It may be helpful to think of a ledger system developing out of the cash book and other ledgers which would have been hand written last century. There would be the cash book containing all cash and/or bank transactions.

As the numbers of customers and suppliers increased there would be many daily invoices out to customers (debtors) and in from suppliers (creditors). It would be necessary and advisable from a practical and control point of view to split up the work of writing up the ledgers.

There would be daily journals (from French *le jour*) or day books which were simply lists of all sales and related sales invoices per day and all purchases and related purchase invoices per day. Ledgers showing who owed money (debtors) and who was owed money (creditors) could be compiled from these lists which were not part of the double entry system, but rather the lists of the raw data from which entries could be made. There would also be the need for a ledger recording fixed assets owned and transactions relating to them. The cash, bank, debtor, creditor and fixed asset ledgers contain details of balance sheet balances and actual physical assets and names of presumably real people and companies – these were traditionally called **real accounts.** The analysed sales and purchase credits and debits or cash expense analysis would be entered in to the appropriate profit and loss account – **nominal accounts or the nominal ledger**. The debtors (also known as sales or accounts receivable) ledger plus the creditors (also known as purchase, bought or accounts payable) ledger plus other real (balance sheet account ledgers) then form the set of ledgers required to record and to be used as a basis for reporting the transactions of the business – they are called the general ledger or total ledger of the business. Although general ledger is the correct term for the entire collection of ledger parts making up the total central records of a business the term nominal ledger is probably more often used.

eg

If the above seems somewhat complicated then a simple diagram of a classic ledger system is as follows (*see over*):

## General or nominal ledger

| Totals of | Balances will typically be debtor/debit | creditor/credit |
|---|---|---|
| **a Fixed assets** | 15,000 | |
| **b Stock** | 1,910 | |
| **c Debtors** | 13,200 | |
| **d Cash/bank** | 1,420 | |
| **e Creditors** | | 11,300 |
| **f Other creditors** | | 1,330 |
| **Share capital** | | X |
| **P & L account** | | X |
| **Sales** | | X |
| **Wages** | X | |
| **Other expenses** | X | |
| | **XXX** = | **XXX** |

**Subsidiary ledgers - containing all the detail**

**Fixed asset register - a**

| | | |
|---|---|---|
| opening balance | 3,000 | |
| new car ref xyz123 | 12,000 | |
| closing balance | 15,000 | |

**Stock records - b**

| | | |
|---|---|---|
| opening balance | 1,300 | |
| transferred 12 Aug | | 290 |
| purchased 14 Aug | 900 | |
| closing balance | 1,910 | |

**Debtors total - c**

| | | |
|---|---|---|
| opening debtors | 12,000 | |
| cash received from debtors | | 9,800 |
| sales to debtors | 11,000 | |
| closing balance | 13,200 | |

**Cash book - d**

| | | |
|---|---|---|
| opening balance | 2,300 | |
| from debtors a/c c | 9,800 | |
| wages 14 Aug | | 2,700 |
| to creditors a/c e | | 6,900 |
| sundry expenses ref pqr | | 120 |
| July PAYE paid | | 970 |
| closing balance | 1,420 | |

**Creditors total - e**

| | | |
|---|---|---|
| opening creditors | | 9,700 |
| cash paid to creditors | 6,900 | |
| purchases on credit | | 8,500 |
| closing balance | | 11,300 |

**Other creditors - f**

| | | |
|---|---|---|
| PAYE July o/s | | 970.00 |
| Bank July PAYE | 970.00 | |
| PAYE for Aug | | 1100.00 |
| Holiday pay accrual | | 230.00 |
| closing balance | | 1,330 |

It is simply the volume of transactions which requires that a general or nominal ledger is split into subsidiary ledgers. It will also be appreciated that if all figures were entered into the general ledger there would be some accounts such as sales, debtors, creditor, wages and of course the cash book which would have thousands of transactions. It makes sense to have all the detail in subsidiary ledgers and what are called control or total accounts in the general ledger.

The term control account is used as routines existed to ensure that the individual postings of say sales, VAT and debtor amounts were entered in the subsidiary ledger and then again independently in total to the control account. At the end of a day, week, month the net balance on the subsidiary ledger could be compared with that in the control account. The balances should of course agree. Nowadays computerised accounting figures are entered once automatically (scanning) or manually, but the figures will be subject to many edit checks for accuracy or at least reasonableness. Also a set of figures on an invoice will not be accepted unless the debits and credits equal.

## Why have internal controls?

The prime reason is to be found in the smallest of businesses – to keep assets safe and not incur unnecessary liabilities or to mirror this, from a profit and loss viewpoint to secure sales (and thus the asset-debtor or cash arising) and control costs.

In the UK and most countries there are no specific laws which require, let alone define the type and numbers of controls which a business should have. It is really left to the owners and directors to decide what are required for business expediency.

It is interesting to note at the time of writing the Hampel report has confirmed what the majority of directors had said, that is it is wrong to insist that details of what are considered to be adequate internal controls should be published in notes to the annual accounts - this had been recommend by the earlier reports on corporate governance. In other words, the directors are appointed to run the business and this includes their making judgements on what are the necessary internal controls.The point being, that assets/liabilities and income and expense can be controlled to the nth degree, at considerable cost, but for what gain?

g

For many industries the nature and levels of control are well established. For example, in the hospitality industry there are well known controls to ensure that all accommodation, food and beverage is paid for. An example of deciding on levels of control and cost versus benefits is to be found in how room mini bars are controlled - a physical stock take is taken daily (the customer can still argue!). On checking out it is often a case of honesty, but in some hotels particularly where labour costs are lower, checkout will phone to have the bar stock checked. An alternative approach is to install mini vending machines - at a cost, but people could still argue - 'I never touched it - honest'!!

From experience as auditor and with many clients of varying size my view would always to be to keep the control as simple as possible - that way you might have a chance of making those that do exist work effectively.

## Other reasons for internal control

*Statutory (non-financial)*

Although there may be no laws requiring financial controls the business may carry out activities for which there is a statutory duty to report transactions (not necessary in currency units). As examples: airlines must record the names and numbers of passengers; the financial services industry must have adequate details of customers and ensure that they are told their rights under current legislation.These examples demonstrate that the need for internal controls is wider than simply financial control.

*To maintain efficient operation/safeguard assets*

Internal controls can assist with ensuring that business processes run smoothly and efficiently, normally by permitting prompt and accurate reports of activity which may then be acted upon.

The known (by employees/customers/suppliers) existence of internal controls often also has a deterrent effect in, for example, that there is less likely to be misappropriation of assets.

Set out on the following pages are descriptions of the typical stages, procedures, controls and documents which are found in accounting systems.

**Sales system or cycle**

**Purchases system or cycle**

**Payroll (wages/salary) system or cycle**

There will also be non trading procedures, general or nominal ledger adjustments.

## Sales system

| Stage/document | Procedures |
|---|---|
| **Sales order** from customer personal/verbal, by phone, in writing | Record order - check credit worthiness |
| **Goods despatched** or services supplied to customer | Goods despatched note - may also act as invoice |
| Invoice raised - printed | Invoice sent to or handed over to customer |
| **Invoice posted** (debits/ and credits entered) | Ledgers updated - typically debtor's individual ledger, debtors' total ledger, sales and VAT output tax |
| **Cash/cheque received** from customer | Debtor's individual account, debtors' total account credited with the received amount, asset cash entered in the cash/bank account. |

**Note:** whilst these are the typical stages and procedures in a sales cycle with computer processing many of the above stages may be combined.

## Purchase system

| Stage/document | Procedures |
|---|---|
| **Requisition** from production or user department in writing or computer generated | Goods/services ordered internally |
| **Goods/services sourced** | Supplier found, supplier appraised for price, quality etc as appropriate |
| Official **order raised** order sent to supplier | Order raised with full details entered on it. Log of orders or commitments maintained |
| **Goods/services received**, goods received note (grn) made out | Goods/services checked for quantity and quality - details entered on a goods received note, or in a log of goods received |
| Supplier invoice received, **invoice registered** | Invoices logged on arrival and subsequent log of invoices maintained |
| **Invoices matched** with order and grn | Matching of invoice/ order/grn to ensure all details correct. Arithmetic and format of supplier invoice checked |
| **Invoice posted** (debits/ and credits entered) | Ledgers updated - typically creditor's individual ledger, creditors' total ledger, cost or expense and VAT input tax |
| **Cheque paid** to customer | Creditor's individual account, creditor's total account debited with the paid amount, bank account balance reduced as cash paid out. |

**Note**: whilst these are the typical stages and procedures in a purchase cycle with computer processing many of the above stages may be combined.

## Wages system

| Stage/document | Procedures |
|---|---|
| **Permanent or standing data** - employee records | Records of employee wage or salary rates, pension deduction rates etc maintained by personnel department |
| Temporary or **transaction data** collected - time sheets or other records of time | Records of work done maintained and details of one-off deductions additions to wage/salary made (and approved) |
| Wage/salary gross, net and **deductions calculated** | Manual or computer calculation and maintenance of individual employee and total wage salary records |
| Total statutory wage/salary deductions **(PAYE, NICs etc)** recorded | |
| **Wage/salary paid** | Payment of wages/salary, usually by bank transfer or cheque. special procedures and controls required for cash payments. |

The outlines (above) are for traditional systems, but even though business operations take many forms and most are computerised, the essential stages remain. More importantly basic controls are still required.

As accounting and internal controls are so important and directors of companies have a responsibility for the proper functioning of what they consider to be adequate internal controls, companies (the finance function) will usually have a detailed record (internal controls memos or manual) of the internal controls to be found operating in the business. An example of the objectives and sub-objectives for a sales cycle is shown below:

## Billing (sales) cycle

*Objective*

**To ensure that all income earned is invoiced, properly recorded as a debtor and is ultimately collected as cash.**

1 **Completeness of orders**

   **Objective**: to ensure that all work done has been ordered (under contract) and all orders are controlled for completeness.

   1.1 All work is proper to the company's business and is controlled from the start

   1.2 No work can go unbilled.

2 **Completeness and timeliness of invoicing**

   **Objective**: to ensure that all work done is invoiced on time/at the earliest time.

   2.1 Projects are billed, and billed on time. Back up control 2.3

   2.2 All invoices are accounted for and details checked for accuracy

   2.3 Back up control over completeness/timeliness of invoicing.

3 **Accuracy of accounting records**

**Objective**: to ensure the completeness, accuracy and validity of entries in the debtors/receivables and general ledgers.

3.1 Sales ledger entries must be as accurate as the invoice details

3.2 Check on completeness and accuracy of invoicing.

4 **Security of the debtor balances and custody recording of cash received**.

**Objective**: to ensure that debtors are recoverable and cash received is properly recorded and kept securely

4.1 Credit worthiness control - therefore control over asset value

4.2 Segregation of duties - cash is kept secure

4.3 Control over security of asset - the debtor. A control over the accuracy of both the posting of invoices and cash receipts.

## Reviewing internal controls

Along with knowledge of the company's reports and accounts and in particular its detailed accounting policies (see Chapter 5 Section 2) it seems a pity that more managers, and certainly surprising, that more directors are not aware of, or have at least an overview of their company's internal control system and procedures.

A simple but revealing method of identifying or selecting necessary controls is to score the worth of procedures and controls.

### Use of scoring system

Firstly, the objectives of the system of internal control must be known.The example above set out the objectives of each stage.These must be to ensure the integrity of financial data, but may include objectives such as timely and accurate recording of units of sales items, controlling staff and customer theft (shrinkage).

A menu of all possible controls found in operation for a specific industry can be drawn up - the relative or actual cost of the different controls should be identified if at all possible.

## Audit function

To most managers the word 'audit' most likely means an external audit carried out by an independent duly authorised auditor or audit may mean internal auditor whose remit is often much wider than that of the external auditor.

### External audit

An external audit is required by law in the UK (with the exception of 'small' companies - those with a turnover less than of £5.6 million) and most other countries where there are limited liability company structures.

The duty of the external auditor is to report to the members of the company - the shareholders - as to whether or not the accounts give a true and fair view and comply with the Companies Acts.The question as to whether the auditors have a duty to a wider audience is one which has been debated over the years and the legal cases have extended then retracted the extent of the duty to others.To the author, as an auditor, who would, naturally, in self interest like any liability limited it does appear odd that if accounts are true and fair, and this is what the shareholders rely on, then why should not others be able to rely on the accounts as well?

## True and fair

What does this mean? Firstly this is a very British term. An auditor would quite rightly never 'certify' accounts in the UK. This is because to us the word certify has the meaning of *confirm absolutely*, and that would be quite impossible to do for every figure in a set of even the simplest accounts.

Leading professionals have said that true and fair cannot be defined - very helpful! In simple terms it means that the accounts are 'true' - correct, ideally to the pence. In practical terms this means within the bounds of materiality. The figures are as exact as practicable in preparation and in substantiation. 'Fair' - means that the presentation of individual figures is conventional, and not in any way aimed to mislead - a simple example would be that if a company has short-term bank deposits of 4m with one bank and an overdraft of 2.5m with another, then it would be quite unfair to show its bank position as 1.5m net cash.

For companies large and small the external auditor will tend to carry out a 'risk based' audit. The auditor should thoroughly know the client, the business, the personnel, the economic conditions as well as the accounting systems and procedures. The auditor will carry out a detailed analytical review and risk assessment during the planning stage to ensure that all risk areas are adequately checked and also that effort is not wasted on low risk areas. The days of checking or vouching large samples of invoices, cheques etc are long gone.

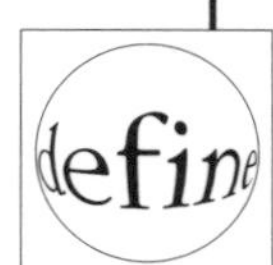

## Internal audit function

Many companies have internal audit departments and these exist for a number of reasons:

- They may be part of the internal control system in that they routinely check processes and transactions
- They may carry out general checking of the accounting systems - they may liaise with the external auditors with a view to reducing the amount of detailed checking which they have to carry out

- They may operate more as an internal consultancy service covering both accounting and general management systems, offering advice on improving the efficiency of operations.

## Directors' responsibilities with respect to accounts

A good summary of directors' responsibilities is to be found in the recommended wording which precedes the auditor's report in statutory accounts:

'The directors are required by the Companies Act 1985 to prepare financial statements for each financial year which give a true and fair view of the state of affairs of the company as at the end of each financial year and of the profit or loss for the financial year.

The directors consider that in preparing the financial statements on pages x to y the company has used appropriate accounting policies, consistently applied and supported by reasonable and prudent judgements and estimates, and that all accounting standards which they consider to be applicable have been followed.

The directors have responsibility for ensuring that the company keeps accounting records which disclose with reasonable accuracy the financial position of the company and which enable them to ensure that the financial statements comply with the Companies Act 1985.

The directors have general responsibility for taking such steps as are reasonably open to them to safeguard the assets of the company and to prevent and detect fraud and other irregularities.'

**This really highlights that all directors should be aware of where the figures come from, how they are compiled and presented. They should also be aware of the internal control systems in operation.**

## Further book keeping examples

| Balance sheet accounts | | | | Profit and loss accounts | | | | |
|---|---|---|---|---|---|---|---|---|
| **Cash** | | | | **Stock for sale - cost of sales** | | | | |
| | Db | | Cr | | Db | | Cr | |
| **balance** | **350** | | | **paid cash** | **300** | | | **The 400 cash balance (debtor) is reduced by the purchase of stock** |
| | | **stock** | **300** | | | | | |

| **Cash** | | | | **Sales** | | | | |
|---|---|---|---|---|---|---|---|---|
| | Db | | Cr | | Db | | Cr | |
| balance | 350 | | | | | **cash received** | **700** | **Customers hand over cash for the stock received by them** |
| | | stock | 300 | | | | | |
| **from** selling | **700** | | | | | | | |

| **Capital** | | | | **The P & L account** | | | | |
|---|---|---|---|---|---|---|---|---|
| | Db | | Cr | | Db | | Cr | |
| | | original* | 350 | **Cost of Sales** | **300** | **Sales** | **700** | **The P & L account is a summary account the profit is the net of sales** |
| | | **profit retained** | **400** | | | | | |
| | | | | **added to capital** | **400** | **profit (credit) balance** | **400** | |

* there must have been original capital of 350 to match the 350 cash balance brought forward

**P & L account**
**for the period ended _ _ _ _ _**

| | |
|---|---|
| **Sales** | **700** |
| **Cost of sales** | **300** |
| **Net profit** | **400** |

**Balance sheet**
**as at _ _ _ _ _ _**

**Assets employed**
**current assets**

| | | |
|---|---|---|
| **Cash** | **750** | original 350 less 300 plus 700 |
| **Financed by** | | |
| **Capital** | **750** | original 350 plus 400 profit retained |

## Further book keeping examples

| a/c number | Balance sheet accounts | | a/c number | Profit and Loss accounts | | |
|---|---|---|---|---|---|---|
| **2020 Bank** | | | | | | |
| | Db | Cr | | | | |
| | **25,000** | | | | | 25,000 invested by shareholders for the business to use - in the bank account - the bank owes 25,000 to the business |
| **4001 Capital** | | | | | | |
| | Db | Cr | | | | 25,000 is the share capital, a liability owed to the shareholders - they would have to liquidate the company to get their money back |
| | | **25,000** | | | | |
| | | | | | | |
| **2020 Bank** | | | | | | |
| | Db | Cr | | | | |
| | **25,000** | | | | | |
| 1001 machine | | **15,000** | | | | 15,000 from the bank spent on a machine - a fixed asset |
| 6001 materials | | **6,000** | | | | |
| | | | **6001 Materials** | | | |
| | | | | Db | Cr | |
| | | | 2020 bank | **6,000** | | 6,000 from the bank spent on materials - part of cost of sales |
| **1001 Fixed asset** | | | 3010 Creditor | **2,500** | | 2,500 material (cost of sales) purchased from a supplier on credit |
| | Db | Cr | | | | |
| | **15,000** | | | | | |
| **3010 Creditor** | | | | | | |
| | Db | Cr | | | | |
| | | **2,500** | | | | |
| | | | | | | |
| **2020 Bank** | | | **6010 Wages** | | | |
| | Db | Cr | | Db | Cr | |
| | **25,000** | | 2020 bank | **2,000** | | 2,000 from the bank spent on wages |
| 1001 machine | | **15,000** | | | | |
| 6001 materials | | **6,000** | | | | |
| 6010 wages | | **2,000** | **7001 Rent** | Db | Cr | |
| 7001 rent | | **1,500** | 2020 bank | **1,500** | | 1,500 from the bank spent on rent 2/3 factory, 1/3 office |
| 7002 electricity | | **700** | | | | |
| | | | **7002 Electricity** | Db | Cr | |
| | | | 2020 bank | **700** | | 700 from the bank spent on electricity - nearly all used in the factory |

**2020 Bank**

| | Db | Cr |
|---|---|---|
| | **25,000** | |
| **1001 machine** | | **15,000** |
| **6001 materials** | | **6,000** |
| **6010 wages** | | **2,000** |
| **7001 rent** | | **1,500** |
| **7002 electricity** | | **700** |
| **5001 sales** | **5,000** | |

**5001 Sales**

| | Db | Cr |
|---|---|---|
| 2020 bank | | **5,000** |
| | | **12,000** |

17,000 of products sold - 5,000 for cash and 12,000 on credit to debtors

**2010 Debtor**

| | Db | Cr |
|---|---|---|
| **5001 Sales** | **12,000** | |

---

**1001 Fixed asset - cost**

| | Db | Cr |
|---|---|---|
| | **15,000** | |

**6091 Depreciation charge**

| | Db | Cr |
|---|---|---|
| 1091 accum depn | **3,000** | |

**1091 Fixed asset - accumulated depreciation**

| | Db | Cr |
|---|---|---|
| 6091 charge for year | | **3,000** |

fixed asset cost remains at what was paid (historically) - 15,000
With expected equal use over a life of 5 years the P&L account is charged with 3,000 and an accumulated depreciation account credited - to recognise consumption of the asset.

---

**2001 Stock**

| | Db | Cr |
|---|---|---|
| 6001 materials | **800** | |

**6001 Materials**

| | Db | Cr |
|---|---|---|
| 2020 bank | **6,000** | |
| 3010 creditor | **2,500** | |
| 2001 stock | | **800** |

not all materials consumed – stock of 800 remains at period end. Materials credited – cost reduced – stock of 800 shown as balance sheet asset-debtor

**Trial balance as at period end**

| account number | Db | Cr |
|---|---|---|
| **1001 Fixed asset** | 15,000 | |
| **1091 Fixed asset - accumulated depreciation** | | 3,000 |
| **2001 Stock** | 800 | |
| **2010 Debtor** | 12,000 | |
| **2020 Bank** | 4,800 | |
| **3010 Creditor** | | 2,500 |
| **4001 Capital** | | 25,000 |
| **5001 Sales** | | 17,000 |
| **6001 Materials** | 7,700 | |
| **6010 Wages** | 2,000 | |
| **6091 Depreciation charge** | 3,000 | |
| **7001 Rent** | 1,500 | |
| **7002 Electricity** | 700 | |
| **totals** | **47,500** | **47,500** |

**Profit and loss account for the period ended**

| | | |
|---|---|---|
| | **Sales** | **17,000** |
| **Cost of sales** | | |
| Materials consumed | 7,700 | |
| Wages | 2,000 | |
| Depreciation | 3,000 | |
| Rent | 1,000 | |
| Electricity | 700 | |
| | | 14,400 |
| | **Gross profit** | **2,600** |
| **Overheads** | | |
| Rent | | 500 |
| | **Net profit** | **2,100** |

**Balance sheet as at**

| | | |
|---|---|---|
| tangible fixed asset - cost | 15,000 | |
| - accumulated depreciation | 3,000 | |
| **fixed assets - net book amount** | | 12,000 |
| **current assets** | | |
| stock | 800 | |
| debtors | 12,000 | |
| bank | 4,800 | |
| | 17,600 | |
| **current liabilities** | | |
| creditor | 2,500 | |
| | 2,500 | |
| **net current assets** | | 15,100 |
| | | 27,100 |
| **Shareholder's equity** | | |
| share capital | | 25,000 |
| profit & loss account | | 2,100 |
| | | 27,100 |

## Checklist

- ✓ Businesses need accounting procedures.
- ✓ Do you know your systems and routines?
- ✓ Businesses need adequate internal controls.
- ✓ Do you know the internal controls which you manage or which affect your reports?
- ✓ Audits can have a positive effect.
- ✓ Do you know the law and legislation which is central to your company's operation?
- ✓ Do you understand your responsibilities as a company director?

section one

# Accounting concepts, policies and standards

## Why do we need concepts and rules?

The great majority of events and transactions are very clear and can be quantified by a very specific amount (of money). The event will clearly indicate whether there is a change in assets/liabilities/income or expense.

For example, if a manufacturer sells equipment which costs 2,700 to manufacture for 4,000 cash, then there is a decrease in equipment finished goods stock of 2,700 an equal P & L cost, sales of 4,000 and an increase in cash of 4,000. The reported profit of 1,300 and asset position in the balance sheet will be indisputably correct.

However, consider if the equipment which cost 2,700 to manufacture was sold to an overseas customer who pays 1,000 by immediate bank transfer and will pay the balance of 3,000 in three months time after delivery and satisfactory performance. The overall figures are as above and the resultant profit and balance sheet figures should be the same.

From today's viewpoint the entire 2,700 stock has gone, replaced by cash of 1,000 and a 3,000 debtor - but is this a 'good' asset - will the customer pay?

It could be argued that income is earned in two stages 1,000 sales today with 3,000 sales in three months, this being confirmed by the customer accepting the item as in working order and paying! Maybe costs would have to be apportioned accordingly as well?

Such situations frequently arise in business and there is thus the need for clear rules as to how to account for and disclose transactions. It is important to realise that there is much convention based on experience, as to how items are disclosed. Although there have been abuses of the conventions with resulting scandals and frauds which have hit the headlines, most businesses are in a position to, and do, report clearly and fairly.

Some accountants and accounting authorities believe that it is possible to be highly prescriptive and set rules - accounting standards and guidelines for every situation. In the UK and in the accounting standards issued by the International Accounting Standards Board (IAS), the view is that rules should be general in nature, leaving the fine detail of rule setting to business entities.

## Fundamental accounting concepts

An early UK accounting standard considered that there were four fundamental accounting concepts:

- Going concern
- Accruals or matching
- Consistency
- Prudence

These are described below as they remain important. The standard setters (US and International – the IASB which issues IAS's and IFRS's) have a 'framework' on which to base accounting standards. This framework recognises Going Concern and Accruals as 'bedrock'. The other two plus other ideas and concepts are considered desirable qualities.

### The four fundamental concepts

*1 Going concern*

The preparer (and auditor) of the accounts should consider and check whether or not the enterprise is likely to continue in operational existence for the foreseeable future. This means in particular that there is no intention or necessity to liquidate or curtail significantly the scale of operations and thus the P & L account and balance sheet will not be materially affected. For example, if a business which manufactures a product line on specialised equipment decides to cease manufacturing the product, the equipment will very likely cease to have and hold the value it did when this part of the business was 'a going concern'.

The 'going concern' concept also requires the preparer (and auditor) to consider and check that the business is likely to have cash/bank resources sufficient to remain in business for the foreseeable future – 'foreseeable future' is considered by UK auditing standards to be at period of at least 12 months beyond the date of signing the latest year end accounts.

*2 Accruals or matching concept*

Revenue and costs should be accrued (that is, recognised as they are earned or incurred, not as money is received or paid), matched with one another so far as their relationship can be established or justifiably assumed, and dealt with in the P & L account of the period to which they relate; with the proviso that where the accruals concept is inconsistent with the 'prudence ' concept the latter will prevail.

*3 Consistency*

There should be consistency of accounting treatment of like items within each accounting period and from one period to the next.

*4 Prudence*

Revenue and thus profits should not be anticipated, but should be recognised by inclusion in the P & L account only when realised either in the form of cash or of other assets which can be realised as cash with reasonable certainty. Provision should be made for all known liabilities (related to expenses and present or future losses) whether the amount of these is known with certainty or is a best estimate in the light of the information available.

## Fundamental concepts in operation

Referring back to the original example – how should the 3,000 (deferred) sale to the overseas customer be accounted for? The fundamental concepts only give guidance. The two which are specifically pertinent in this case are the accruals and prudence concepts. From a timing (accruals or matching) point of view is it correct to recognise the sale today? Probably yes, stock has been sold (there should be paper work, a contract or at least an order and sales invoice).The further matter to consider is the quality of the 3,000 debtor - will the customer have a reason or find an excuse not to accept the equipment? Will the customer pay? Is it prudent to accept the 3,000 as an asset. It may be necessary (prudent) to make some provision against the debtor not paying. This does raise the question as to why goods were sold to this customer in the first place!

The fundamental concepts are the basis from which detailed accounting policies are developed. Two frequently met situations where accounting policies are required are - depreciation of fixed assets and valuation of stock/ inventory and work in progress (WIP).

### Depreciation

The exercise of depreciating a fixed asset is the operation of the matching concept. By definition a fixed asset is one that lasts for and is in use in more than one accounting period. It is a long-term asset in the balance sheet. The fixed asset is used or consumed over its life and loses value. If nothing is done about recognising the use, the asset will still be shown in the balance sheet with value - it is a 'phoney' asset. The exercise of depreciating assets is one of **matching** their use over their expected life. A simple example of the arithmetic of depreciation was shown on page 140 in Chapter 4 Section 2.

fixed asset cost 15,000

zero value at end of 5 years

expected useful life 5 years - assumed to be used an equal amount each year of its working life

annual depreciation charge 15,000/5 = 3,000 per year

The cost of the asset can therefore be matched with the benefit/income arising from using it.

## Stock/WIP valuation

The exercise of counting or taking stock at the end of an accounting period is again the **matching** concept in action. A simple example of the arithmetic of the stock adjustment was shown on page 140 in Chapter 4 Section 2.

| | |
|---|---|
| materials purchased in the period | 8,500 |
| stock held at the end of the period | 800 |
| therefore materials consumed into products in the period | 7,700 |

It would be incorrect to show all the materials purchased as a cost of production, those not taken into production or sold are an asset of the business, not a cost. This is of course assuming the stock does hold value and can be used or realised in the next accounting period.

A question arises over what figure to use for the value of stock? In the simple example above the conventional and normally correct figure is the cost of the remaining stock or WIP should be valued at what it cost.

However, if for some reason the stock on hand had deteriorated or could be replaced at a (permanently) much lower price, then the stock should be written down to its net realisable value (nrv). This is the **prudence** concept in operation.

It is obvious that if the stock has deteriorated then it will not realise so much when ultimately sold. Equally if it was possible to purchase replacement stock at a much lower price then the stock held will not realise so much or maybe even its original cost on ultimate sale.

Much can be made of what is the cost of stock or WIP. If stock items are purchased piecemeal over time then what is the cost of the stock at the period end? In the UK it is generally accepted that stock should be accounted for and therefore valued on a 'first in first out basis' (FIFO), that is remaining stock is the most recently purchased. This seems entirely reasonable as stock will be at an up to date cost. Also it is likely that the oldest stock will be sold first.

With the possible range of figures, and particularly opinions as to what the cost or ultimate selling price might be, it will be appreciated that stock/WIP valuation is a critical area for preparers of accounts and auditors. Stock valuation is often a highly subjective area.

## Accounting policies

The fundamental accounting concepts are used as a basis for preparing the rules or accounting policies to be applied when preparing a set of accounts.

For many businesses there is no great issue over the use of the fundamental concepts and rules - accounting policies based thereon. A small trading company would typically have the following accounting policies, often as the first note to the accounts.

**XYZ Limited**

*Notes to the accounts for the year ended 31 March 2xx7*

**Accounting policies**

*Accounting convention*

**The accounts are prepared under the historical cost convention.**

This simply means that the figures, particularly balance sheet assets, are based on what the respective item cost, there has been no revaluation of any item. This is quite correctly prudent for current assets, but may be misleading for tangible fixed assets and thus a policy of revaluing land and buildings may be adopted.

*Turnover*

**Turnover represents the invoiced amounts of goods sold and services provided net of value added or sales tax.**

This makes it clear that the sales income shown is that of the business and does not include the VAT or sales tax element of sales which has to go to the government.

*Depreciation*

**Depreciation is provided on all tangible fixed assets at rates calculated to write off the cost or valuation of each asset over its expected useful life as follows:**

| | |
|---|---|
| *Motor vehicles* | *4 years* |
| *Fixtures and Fittings* | *10-50 years* |
| *Electronic Equipment* | *3 years* |

This sets out the rates (not highly detailed) by which fixed asset cost is spread over time - the accruals or matching principle.

*Stocks*

**Stocks are stated at the lower of cost or net realisable value.**

This states that stocks are valued at what they cost, not revalued in any way, further if the stock is now not worth so much - it has deteriorated or 'gone off' it is written down to the net amount which should be realised - the prudence concept.

There is really nothing very deep or controversial in the above and these policies are typical for a small business. Not all business operations will be simple and more detailed, specific policies will be required. Again, in the published accounts the meaning and effect of policies should be clear.

### Read the accounting policies

The reason for reviewing the accounting policies is that the figures in the accounts can only really be properly interpreted if the base upon which they are prepared is known. With the majority of figures there will be no problem, but there may be figures which are prepared and disclosed in an unconventional manner. The policies must be reviewed before looking at the figures.

### Accounting policies should relate to the business (be appropriate for the business)

What policies are needed, what are appropriate? You do not need to be an accountant to appreciate that policies should be appropriate to the type of business being carried out.

For example, from a telecommunications company accounts as illustrated earlier.

*Engineering stores*

eg

*Most engineering stores items are used in the construction of new plant and the remainder for maintenance. When issued these stores are charged to the cost of the specific plant or to the profit and loss account as appropriate. They are stated at cost, less a provision for excess and obsolete items.*

A policy which clearly states that costs of equipment is correctly allocated as asset or cost when taken from stores. Also stores are valued on a prudent basis.

Further and more detailed analysis of accounting policies can be found in Section 2.

## Checklist

- ✓ Income and expenses should be matched.
- ✓ Figures should be prepared and disclosed in a prudent and consistent manner.
- ✓ Accounting policies should be studied before the figures.
- ✓ Accounting policies should relate to the business.

# Accounting concepts, policies and standards

Accounting standards

Detailed accounting policies

Developing accounting policies

A contractor

A travel agency

Creative accounting

Creative accounting illustration

Checklist

## Accounting standards

It is not the place of this text to give a history of accounting standards or carry out a comparative study of the standards to be found in different countries. Set out below is a brief background to the UK and International Financial Reporting Standards - IFRS's (but formerly called International Accounting Standards - IAS's) along with a précis of the purpose of the principal standards.

### Background to accounting standards

The setting of standards is a comparatively recent event. For decades there have been accepted concepts and conventions but no formal rules and standards. In fact it was not until the 1970's that Britain had its first standards.

There was much convention as to the bases, layout and disclosure of figures and statements but company law did not prescribe the manner in which figures should be calculated or disclosed.

It should be noted that the UK and US approach (based on a common law background) differs from say the French approach (based on a code law system - the Napoleonic Code).The disclosure requirements in various countries are affected by many factors, the legal system as mentioned above, the history of trade development and the economic structure - free enterprise versus centrally planned.

With the dominant position of US companies and with the globalisation of trade, the US standards (GAAP - Generally Accepted Accounting Practices) are the greatest in number and detail. Other countries, particularly the UK, developed their own standards (many being similar in principal to the US standards) and contributed to the setting up of a body, the International Accounting Standards Board (IASB). The IASB produces international standards which meet the needs of each participating country and, more importantly, national stock exchanges around the world.This independent body, comprising members from national accounting bodies, had its authority boosted by the EU legislating that the standards called International Financial Reporting Standards (IFRS's) be compulsory for listed companies operating in Europe.

The IASB, the UK, the US and other standard setting countries are moving to converge their respective standards.

## Legal force of standards

The Companies Act 1985 clearly implies that accounts should be prepared in accordance with accepted accounting standards and Schedule 4 to the Act describes the use of fundamental accounting concepts. Accounting standards are issued by the Accounting Standards Board (ASB) in the UK and are the 'law' as far as any qualified accountant or registered auditor is concerned. There was debate over whether or not Standards should be set by and their use governed by the profession. The ASB is now part of the Financial Reporting Council which has a high degree of independence and thus it is fair to say that UK Standards are impartially prepared and properly monitored in use.

The need to follow standards may be enshrined in law but possibly the more important need is to meet stock exchange requirements – if there is inadequate or improper disclosure, a company's shares will not be listed on a recognised stock market. It is also the force of the markets which was behind the drive to have an agreed set of International Financial Reporting Standards. If companies wish to raise new equity capital, they will have to comply with disclosure requirements demanded by recognised stock markets.

## Purpose and content of principal accounting standards

The purpose of the UK, US and international standards is above all to bring consistency of reporting. Other reasons are to ensure 'full' disclosure, that is, no hidden or undervalued assets or, more importantly, hidden or understated liabilities. There is also the need for standards to assist in disclosing transactions where there may be several interpretations of events. A general point of principal is that with disclosure of figures and related notes there should be an emphasis on 'substance over form', that is, the commercial reality of transitions and resulting assets/ liabilities should be shown rather than that required by a strict interpretation of (the minimum) legally required disclosure.

It is beyond the scope of this text to précis or even list all extant UK or international standards. If a reader has a particular problem with disclosure of balance sheet or P & L items, reference to UK or international standards is quite likely to reveal that there is a standard covering the item. For example, there are several standards covering tangible fixed assets, investment fixed assets, stocks and work-in-progress. There are also standards covering the fundamental concepts and balance sheet and P & L disclosures.

## Detailed accounting policies

Generally the published accounting policies are glib - there is not the space to go into great detail and it may be that too much detail would confuse the average reader of the accounts.

As stated in Section 1, most accounting policies are conventional and this is another reason why many published notes may appear glib. On reviewing policies what you are looking for is the unusual, those that seem out of line with the type of business apparently being carried on or which are 'loose' - that is permit a wide range of interpretations.

Set out below are accounting policies notes taken from the published accounts of various companies in different industry sectors.

Each note is followed by a commentary on what it means and highlighting critical points, if any.

### Construction company

*Provision is made at current prices for the cost of restoring land from which minerals have been extracted.*

The liability to reinstate land used for quarrying is being acknowledged. The question to be asked would be, 'Is adequate provision being made?' Current prices are being used - will the standards of reinstatement not be higher by the time the work has to be carried out?

### Long-term contracts

*Amounts recoverable on contracts, which are included in debtors, are stated at cost plus attributable profit less any foreseeable losses. Payments received on account of contracts are deducted from amounts recoverable on contracts. Such amounts which have been received and exceed amounts recoverable are included in creditors.*

This policy follows UK SSAP 9. Profitable work done on projects is considered as sold and thus a debtor in the balance sheet. If the cost of work done and to be done is in excess of likely sales, the expected loss is provided for now. The cash received from the customer is netted against the debtor in the balance sheet or, if in excess (advance payments from the customer), the payments in advance are shown in the balance sheet as a liability - due back to the customer. This is obviously prudent.

## Airport owner and operator

*Fixed assets*

**1 Investment properties**

*Fully completed properties let to, and operated by, third parties and held for long-term retention, including those at airport locations, are accounted for as investment properties and valued at the balance sheet date at open market value. All investment properties are revalued annually and by external valuers at least once every five years. Any surplus or deficit in revaluation is transferred to revaluation reserve except that deficits below original cost which are expected to be permanent are charged to the profit and loss account.*

*Profits or losses arising from the sale of investment properties are calculated by reference to book value and treated as exceptional items.*

*In accordance with SSAP 19, Accounting for Investment Properties, no depreciation is provided in respect of freehold or long-term leasehold investment properties. This is a departure from the Companies Act 1985 which requires all properties to be depreciated. Such properties are not held for consumption but investment and the directors consider that to depreciate them would not give a true and fair view. Depreciation is only one amongst many factors reflected in the annual valuation of properties and accordingly the amount of depreciation which might otherwise have been charged cannot be separately identified or quantified. The directors consider that this policy results in the accounts giving a true and fair view.*

Those properties defined as investment properties (rather than being tangible fixed assets used directly by the company) are being regularly revalued (up or down) with periodic independent back-up to the valuations – this is simply good business and accounting practice.

Company law picked up the point that tangible fixed assets do wear out or are consumed and thus requires that they be depreciated. SSAP 19 acknowledges that investment properties are considered as investments and not used directly by the owning company and therefore depreciation is considered inappropriate and the true and fair view is given by not depreciating.

### 2 Operational assets

*Terminal complexes, airfield assets, plant and equipment, fixtures and fittings and group occupied properties are stated at cost less accumulated depreciation. Assets in course of construction are stated at cost less provision for permanent diminution in value and assume that projects in early planning stages will receive consents necessary to achieve a successful outcome. Where appropriate, cost includes interest, own labour and associated overheads.*

Other tangible fixed assets are stated at (historical) cost. This includes capitalised interest and the cost of the company's own labour and associated overheads. The questions to be asked would be, 'How much interest is capitalised?' this can usually be found in a note to the accounts; 'How much 'own work' has been capitalised and what is the amount of overhead included in this cost?'

### 3 Depreciation

*Depreciation is provided on operational assets, other than land, to write off the cost of the assets by equal instalments over their useful lives as follows:*

***Fixed assets lives***

| | |
|---|---|
| *Terminal building, pier and satellite structures* | *50 years* |
| *Terminal fixtures and fittings* | *5-20 years* |
| *Airport plant and equipment including runway lighting and building plant* | *5-20 years* |
| *Tunnels, bridges and subways* | *50 years* |
| *Runways, taxiways and aprons* | *up to 100 years* |

*Transit systems:*

| | |
|---|---|
| *- rolling stock* | *20 years* |
| *- track* | *50 years* |
| *Motor vehicles* | *4-8 years* |
| *Office equipment* | *5-10 years* |
| *Short leasehold properties* | *over the period of the lease* |

*Major periodic maintenance expenditure on runways, taxiways and aprons is charged to the profit and loss account as incurred.*

A policy stating the method of depreciation - straight line and giving a fairly detailed indication of the lives of the tangible fixed assets.

### Properties held for resale

*Properties held for resale are stated at the lower of cost and net realisable value.*

This policy indicates that these properties are really treated as trading stock.

### Interest

*Interest payable is charged as incurred, except when the borrowing finances tangible fixed assets in the course of construction. Such interest is capitalised once planning permission has been obtained and a firm decision to proceed has been taken until the asset is complete and income-producing and then written off by way of depreciation of the relevant asset.*

This policy reiterates the practice of capitalising interest borrowings related to capital expenditure on major new fixed assets.

### The oil corporation

#### Environmental conservation and site restoration cost

*Liabilities for environmental conservation are recorded when it is probable that obligations have been incurred and the amounts can reasonably be estimated. These liabilities are not reduced by possible recoveries from third parties and projected cash expenditures are not discounted.*

*Site restoration costs that may be incurred by the Corporation at the end of the operating life of certain of its facilities and properties are reserved rateably over the asset's productive life.*

The liabilities for environmental related costs is being acknowledged. The charge is being made rateably (proportionally) over the life of the asset (to be decommissioned). The question which must be asked is, 'Is adequate provision being made?' What will the environmental standards be when the site/plant is finally decommissioned?

### Supermarket chain plc

#### Basis of financial statements

*The financial statements have been prepared in accordance with applicable accounting standards, under the historical cost convention, and are in accordance with the Companies Act 1985.*

The historical cost basis is being used - figures are at cost or net realisable value if lower. There is no revaluation of properties. This can be compared with the airport owner and operator policy on page 158.

#### Stocks

*Stocks are valued on the basis of first in first out at the lower of cost and net realisable value. Stocks in stores are calculated at retail prices and reduced by appropriate margins to the lower of cost and net realisable value.*

Stocks are correctly being valued at cost or net realisable value on first in first out basis (FIFO), that is, it is assumed that the oldest items are sold first. Let's hope so! Strictly speaking, stock should be counted and valued at invoiced (purchased) cost. This would be quite impractical for a supermarket business - the retail price of merchandise is clearly known as are very precise margins by which the retail prices may be reduced to cost.

## A telecommunication company

*VII Intangible assets*

*Broadcasting licences, which are held in an associated undertaking, are stated at historical cost. No amortisation is provided on these assets, but their value is reviewed annually by the directors and the cost is written down if permanent diminution in value has occurred.*

The intangibles are not owned directly by the company or a subsidiary but rather in an associate. The value in the associate's accounts is historical cost or net realisable value - this is prudent, but the question to be asked is, 'Are these intangibles worth considerably more than historic cost?'

As an example of what is meant, set out below are the accounting policies of the hotel chain, followed by a summary explanation of what they mean. Some of the policies are quite detailed and the meaning may be obscure, for example, consolidation and deferred tax. At this stage accept that these do just explain normal accounting convention. If you encounter unclear wording, hopefully you should be able to get an accountant to clarify the situation!

## Question

Review the following accounting policies - which one(s) require more explanation?

## Accounting policies

*1 Accounting convention*

The accounts have been prepared under the historical cost convention as modified by revaluations of certain properties and investments, and in accordance with the Companies Act 1985, as amended by the Companies Act 1989, and applicable Accounting Standards.

*2 Basis of consolidation*

a) **Acquisitions and disposals.** The Group balance sheet includes all the assets and liabilities of subsidiary undertakings including those acquired during the period. The Group profit on ordinary activities after taxation includes only that proportion of the results arising since the effective date of control, or in the case of undertakings or interests disposed of, for the period of ownership.

b) **Associated undertakings.** The Group profit on ordinary activities before taxation includes the Group's proportion of the profits and losses of associated undertakings and the taxation charge includes taxation on those results.

c) **Joint ventures.** The results and net assets of joint ventures are fully consolidated where the Group has a participating interest therein and either manages them on a unified basis with certain subsidiary undertakings or actually exercises dominant influence over them.

d) **Goodwill.** Goodwill represents the difference between the costs of acquisition and the fair value of the separable net assets acquired. Goodwill is written off or credited to reserves in the year of acquisition.

e) **Overseas undertakings.** The Group accounts are prepared in accordance with UK generally accepted accounting principles.

### 3 Sales

Sales represent the amounts receivable for services provided and goods sold, excluding inter-group sales, VAT and similar sales taxes.

### 4 Interest, internal professional fees and preopening expenses

Interest on capital employed on the construction and major development of hotels and restaurants and internal professional costs incurred until these enterprises start to trade may, if appropriate, be capitalised as part of the costs of construction. In addition, pre-opening and development expenses incurred up to the start of full trading may, if appropriate, be deferred and written off over five to ten years.

### 5 Fixed assets

a) **Property values.** Freehold properties and leasehold properties with twenty years or more to run at the balance sheet date are revalued at regular intervals and the resultant valuation is included in the balance sheet. When the unexpired term falls below twenty years, no further revaluations are carried out.

b) **Revaluation reserve.** The difference between the resultant valuation and historic cost is recorded in the revaluation reserve to the extent that the valuation exceeds historic cost on a property by property basis. Any permanent diminution in the value of fixed assets is charged to the profit and loss account as appropriate after making any associated adjustment) to the revaluation reserve.

c) **Disposals.** Where the Group disposes of fixed assets in the normal course of trading, the profit or loss arising is included in the profit on ordinary activities before taxation. The profit or loss on disposal is calculated by reference to the revalued amount.

d) **Depreciation of properties.** In accordance with normal practice in the UK hotel industry, no depreciation is provided on freehold properties or properties on leases with twenty years or more to run at the balance sheet date or on integral fixed plant. It is the Group's practice to maintain these assets in a continual state of sound repair and to extend and make improvements thereto from time to time. Accordingly the Directors consider that the lives of these assets and residual values (based on prices prevailing at the time of acquisition or subsequent valuation) are such that their depreciation) is insignificant. All leasehold properties held for less than twenty years are amortised over the unexpired term.

e) **Depreciation of other assets.** Depreciation is provided on all other assets on a straight line basis over ten to fifteen years for plant and machinery, four to ten years for furniture and equipment and up to five years for information technology software and hardware.

### 6 Leases

Finance leases are those which transfer substantially all the risks and rewards of ownership to the lessee. Assets held under such leases are capitalised as tangible fixed assets and depreciation is provided where appropriate. Outstanding finance lease obligations which comprise principal plus accrued interest, are included within creditors falling due after more than one year. The finance element of the agreements is charged to the profit and loss account over the term of the lease on a systematic basis. All other leases are operating leases. The rentals on such leases are charged to the profit and loss account as incurred.

### 7 Stocks

Stocks are stated at the lower of cost and net realisable value.

*8 Pensions*

The cost of providing pensions and other post retirement benefits is charged against profits on a systematic basis with pension surpluses and deficits arising allocated over the expected remaining service lives of employees.

*9 Deferred taxation*

Provision is made for deferred taxation arising from timing differences between profits as computed for taxation purposes and profits as stated in the accounts to the extent that the liability will be payable in the foreseeable future.

*10 Foreign currencies*

Overseas trading results are expressed in sterling at the average rates of exchange ruling during the financial year. Overseas net assets and UK loans denominated in foreign currencies are expressed in sterling at the average rates of exchange ruling during one week prior and one week subsequent to the balance sheet date or contracted sales where appropriate. The effect of currency movements on assets and liabilities is taken to reserves.

**Answer**

**Review of the hotel chain's accounting policies**

*1 Accounting convention*

Historical cost basis. This means that the accounts are prepared with historical figures, that is the figures arising whenever a transaction occurred. This is the accepted convention as it would be unrealistic to continually revalue, say machinery or stocks. In any event many figures such as debtors, creditors and loan balances will not change just because of the passage of time.

However, it is generally recognised as good practice to revalue properties. Properties have tended to significantly increase in value over the years. Normal commercial property can usually be valued with a fair degree of accuracy and it thus makes sense to show an up to date value – there is more worth for the shareholders and more security for borrowing purposes.

### 2 Basis of consolidation

These notes set out the general basis on which the accounts of all the companies in the group are drawn together – consolidated.

d) Goodwill.This indicates an ultra prudent approach in that any premium paid on acquisition of a subsidiary is written off immediately. For years this was the accepted method in the UK, more recently a policy of writing goodwill off over periods of up to 20 years was adopted. Today both UK GAAP and IFRS's require goodwill to be carried in the balance sheet at the cost or purchase amount. The goodwill figure is then checked annually for 'impairment'. Impairment means – has the value declined in which case the write down is debited to the P&L account or income statement – there is a 'hit' against profits.

Impairment can come about because of market changes, technological changes, expiry of a patent or simply lack of support for (advertising) the brands etc which make up the intangible goodwill value.

### 3 Sales

A very conventional policy. Only sales to third parties are included net of VAT and sales taxes which belong to the appropriate revenue authority.

### 4 Interest, internal professional fees and pre-opening expenses

This is the interesting one! What some might consider normal costs incurred in developing a business are possibly included as part of fixed assets, rather than being charged to the P & L account. The use of words like 'may', 'if appropriate''full trading' require further explanation. Exactly how much is being deducted from costs and classified as assets? Are these costs real assets?

*5 Fixed assets to ten foreign currencies*

These are all quite conventional policies, but for 5(d) strictly speaking business, as opposed to investment properties should be depreciated.

## Developing accounting policies

### Accounting policies within the company

There is obviously the over-riding need to comply with published accounting standards. In doing so there will often be the need to set out in some detail how events, transactions and the related figures are compiled and reported internally as well as in the published accounts.

### Detailed accounting policies, accounting instructions and manuals

All companies, even the smallest, should have written accounting policies available for all those who are expected to take responsibility for reports and figures. This is not a matter of bureaucracy, but rather to ensure that everyone who deals with and has to act on figures knows on what they are based.

It often seems a waste that all the thought and effort by accountants which has gone into devising appropriate detailed accounting policies is not more widely used or at least explained to the directors and managers of companies.

Properly formulated and actioned practical accounting policies can assist in the proper running of the business, also bringing consistency to resulting actions.

Even for small companies it may be useful to review and commit to writing accounting policies in some detail – they often tie in with the accounting procedures, routines and controls which ought to be found in any business. There is also a link with ISO 9000 certification.

Set out below are two short extracts from accounting manuals. It is impracticable to give examples of all the detailed policies which would be required for all types of business. These paragraphs are meant as an illustration of what should exist in any organisation and of which many managers should be more aware.

## A contractor

### Sales profit recognition

*Definition of types of sale*

The accounting policy reflects the fact that all XYZ plc projects can be defined as being either

A **Direct Sales Projects (DS)**

or

B **Earned Value Projects (EV)**

*Accounting Policies*

**A D S Projects**

The policy is to recognise a sale and thus the profit when the project work is invoiced.

Project work will only be invoiced when clear deliverables can and will be acknowledged by the customer. At this point the sales value is clearly known and costs relating to the sale can fully and clearly be identified and thus the profit accurately measured.

**B EV Projects**

The policy is to recognise income and profit prudently as the work is done – as costs are incurred on the project.

Earned Value is calculated monthly, based on the full costs of the project plus the appropriate expected profit margin. Basing the calculation on the costs to date means that the costs to date have to result in useful, saleable work done and this position is critically reviewed during the Project Review Process.

The above policy is only an outline and more detail is required.

## A travel agency

### Sales and deposits

Revenue is to be recognised on a prudent basis – when it has been indisputably earned.

### Deposits

Deposits are of two types – refundable and non-refundable.

*Accounting procedures*

All deposits received, whether refundable or not, should be entered in the daily cash received sheets and full details recorded as liabilities of the business in deposit creditor accounts C564 and C565.

*Accounting policy – revenue recognition*

At the end of each month the deposit creditor account, non refundable deposits, C565 print out should be reviewed (by the office manager) to confirm that all entries are in respect of non-refundable deposits and that no known disputes exist over any of the balances. On completion of this the credit balance on the account can be released to P & L account S120 as income for the month. Any likely to be disputed balances should be transferred to disputed deposits account C569 to remain as liability balances.

## Commission arising on air and rail ticket sales

*Accounting procedures*

All ticket sales income should be credited in full to the operators account in the creditors ledger K123 to K129.

The company's calculation of commission income earned for the month should be debited to contra account K199 and credited to P & L current commission account S139. These entries are to be reversed out at the end of each month when the next month's estimates are entered and the actual agreed commission is credited to the P & L account.

On receipt of the operators' agreed commission income for the previous month, the commission amount can be released to P & L account S130.

*Accounting policy*

The procedures above ensure that only agreed commission is recognised as income at any month end. At the financial year end a full review of the commission calculation exercise should be carried out by the office manager.

**The above procedures and policies are clearly prudent and fairly detailed. It is important to understand exactly how they would operate in practice and again any accounting procedures and policy manual should have examples of the forms and accounts referred to.**

## Creative accounting

The term 'creative accounting' often excites interest and undoubtedly there have been many instances.

A major task of standard setters is seen to be to prevent or outlaw such practices, to ensure that accounts give a clear view of the substance of the transactions they purport to present rather than just the often minimum, purely legally required disclosure. Creative accounting can go further and be an exercise in hiding what is going on. Obviously the boundaries between creative accounting and fraud must at times be vague. The intent of the creative accountant needs to be known – is it just paranoia with secrecy or a deliberate intention to deceive?

There are many ways of being creative or misrepresenting events and transactions. Common bases for creative accounting are as follows:

### Lacking prudence

This may be the concept to rely on if you want to get away with creative accounting! Prudence is very often highly subjective and a 'lighter' view on what is prudent can give better results – lower costs (accrued) or higher income recognise.A good test of whether or not there is any creativity is to check what conventional practice is among respected companies.

### Mis matching

If clear mis matches are detected, then this may be pushing the boundaries of being creative towards being fraudulent. Examples from the past are receipts or deposits for future work or services being recorded and reported as income rather than correctly as deferred income – creditor or liability balances.

### Being inconsistent

This should be rather blatant but inconsistencies could be hidden.

### Netting off – window-dressing

Netting off means hiding items by showing them included with other balances and only showing the net figure. An example of netting off in the balance sheet - 'window-dressing' - the balance sheet would be to show a six month money market deposit of say 4m netted against an overdraft of 7m to give a net 3m overdraft - this is not the true position!

### Taking items off balance sheet

This has been an objective of many, and means removing assets and, more significantly, related borrowings/loans from a balance sheet. The aims are to show a slimmer company - less capital employed and to hide the extent of borrowings/loans and future commitments to repay the loans. This (along with inflating income) was a major feature of the Enron case.

In the UK Accounting Standards on leases and UK Financial Reporting Standard (FRS) 5 - Substance of Transactions are aimed at preventing off balance sheet transactions.

The US standard covering off balance vehicles and transactions was somewhat legalistic and contributed to the 'clever' Enron accounting. The Enron debacle may have been a good thing as it has helped in the recognition that 'principles' based, as opposed to 'rules' based, standards may be more effective. That is if you have rules for every eventuality then there is the challenge to get round the rules - clear principles might be better.

## Creative accounting illustration

### Nadir Networks plc

The following notes to the accounts and notes to the balance sheet demonstrate what might be done.

The small company had prudent accounting policies in respect of its expenditure in developing computer software - all costs were written off as incurred. Also the moneys it received in respect of warranties for computer hardware servicing were treated as a liability in the year they were received and were only released to the P&L account as income at the end of the year when there was no further liability to the customer to repair equipment - again a very prudent policy.

As relatively substantial sums were being expended on developing software it was considered that 'know-how' was being acquired and thus the costs were more of the nature of an intangible fixed asset. The accounting policy was thus changed to permit the capitalisation of a proportion of development cost. The resulting intangible asset was then to be depreciated or amortised over a period of three years - really quite prudent!

In the year concerned, the company set up a new subsidiary to carry out the warranty repair work and thus took the view that instead of showing moneys received as liabilities they could now take these as income as long as they made adequate provision for any likely repair costs - still a prudent approach!

The net effect of the above was to bring credits of some 67,000 to the P&L account - all through legitimately changing the accounting policies - the changes certainly created profit.

It should be noted that all of this is disclosed in the accounts and notes, and it could be said that it is up to the reader of the accounts to take note. Where there are changes in accounting policies, this fact should be highlighted and the effect of the changes separately noted, restating previous figures to show what they would have been had the new policies been in effect last year.

## Nadir Networks plc

*Notes to the Accounts at 30 September 2xx5*

*1 Accounting Policies*

**Accounting Convention**

The accounts are prepared under the historical cost convention.

**Turnover**

Turnover represents the invoiced amounts of goods sold and services provided net of value added tax.

**Software Development**

Once it is certain that expenditure on development of software is matched by income at such a value and in such volume that development costs are likely to be recovered, expenditure (comprising mainly salaries) is capitalised and then written off over a prudent period (4 years).

**Depreciation**

Depreciation is provided on all tangible fixed assets at rates calculated to write off the cost or valuation of each asset over its expected useful life as follows:

| | |
|---|---|
| Motor vehicles | 4 years |
| Fixtures and Fittings | 10-50 years |
| Electronic Equipment | 3 years |

**Stocks**

Stocks are stated at the lower of cost or net realisable value.

### Balance sheet notes

**6 Intangible Assets – Software**

| | | 2xx4 |
|---|---|---|
| | £ | £ |
| Capitalised | 65,038 | 29,038 **a** |
| Amortisation | 10,000 | – |
| Net Book Amount | 55,038 | 29,038 |

**9 Creditors: Amounts falling due within one year**

| | | 2xx4 |
|---|---|---|
| | £ | £ |
| Overdraft | 92,771 | 101,943 |
| Creditors and Accruals | 66,602 | 91,346 |
| Accrued Income/ Provision for Maintenance | 8,000 | 21,140 **b** |
| Other Taxes | 30,394 | 30,280 |
| HP Liability | 9,231 | 10,286 |
| Directors' Loans | 46,880 | 14,480 |
| | 253,878 | 269,475 |

a The costs have been capitalised and the net effect for 1995 is a net 55,038 reduction in costs. 10,000 was taken from costs for the previous year.

b There was no note on the change in policy for the warranty income – maybe it was considered immaterial! The detail on current liabilities shows the scale of the change, instead of accruing some 20,000 of income, only 8,000 is accrued as being the costs of servicing the remaining warranties.

## Checklist

- ✓ Accounting standards exist and have to be complied with.
- ✓ Know the principals of the standards which affect the reporting of your business.
- ✓ Accounting policies are a basis for you to understand your figures.
- ✓ Do you need to know your own detailed accounting policies?
- ✓ Do you need to get involved in developing your own detailed accounting policies?

*section one*

# Interpretation

## Ratio analysis

## Checklist

# Ratio analysis

## How do you measure the performance of a business?

The first point which normally comes to mind is profitability - the business must make a profit.

Another point, maybe closer to the heart of the smaller business is, does the business generate positive cash flows, or at least sufficient cash to survive? This is also important to all companies, particularly listed companies as there is a need to pay regular cash dividends - there is of course an underlying need to generate profit!

Again, for all sizes of business without profits (and positive cash flows) there will be no funds to invest in new assets and business growth.

Yet another measure of performance may be seen as in general efficiency - how well does the business use its assets - do the managers 'make the assets sweat'?

There are also many non financial measures of performance which may well have an effect on the level of financial performance. For example, staff turnover or the frequency of environmental law infringements - surely these must have an impact on results!

## The need to make an adequate return

The prime measure of a business' success, or not, is the level of return on the capital employed. It is a ratio of the profit the business makes divided by the capital employed to deliver the profit.

It is the level of net operating profit (return) in relation to either the capital employed by, or invested in, the business (the net assets employed or equity and loans which fund the net assets).

This could be considered as follows. You have £100,000 invested in plant and machinery, stock, etc, and this can be used to manufacture and sell items, the profit at the end of a period divided by the £100,000 will be the return on the capital employed.

In simple terms, this is similar to saying that if you have £100,000 invested in a bank deposit account and interest of £9,800 is earned over a period of a year, the return on capital employed is

$$\frac{9{,}800}{100{,}000} = 9.8\%$$

There are innumerable figures produced by businesses every day, thus the possibility of analysis of figures is endless. Basic analysis of figures using a business or balance sheet and P & L account yields important information which will reflect the nature of the business being analysed, also how it is performing in relation to other similar businesses. This section describes the principal financial ratios used in measuring or comparing business performance.

A business must above all deliver results, not just one-off results but improving or at least consistent results over a number of years. The return which can be achieved or delivered will depend on the results (profits) and this return will be equated with market norms.The prime ratio is called the return on capital employed (ROCE). It is also known as return on investment (ROI), return on net assets (RONA) and equals the net operating profit divided by capital employed.

The return which a business delivers must, over the years, satisfy the providers of funds invested in the business.What rate is appropriate may be considered a matter for economists but typically rates which have been achieved by UK and US companies will be as high as 20%.The rate will be considerably lower for countries such as Japan and Germany where 8% might be considered satisfactory.There is, of course, a relationship between the rate providers of capital require and the interest rates prevailing in the economies of the countries concerned. Further, the interest rates in the countries will be linked to the rate of inflation in the countries.

The prime measure of performance is:

$$\textbf{Return on capital employed} = \frac{\textbf{Net operating profit}}{\textbf{Capital employed}}$$

**Net operating profit** is normally taken as net operating profit of the ordinary on-going business before interest and taxation.

**Capital employed** is taken as the year end or average capital employed in generating the profit.

It is obvious that return on capital employed could be calculated either before or after tax and interest.The figure which is used for calculation will depend very much on the reasons for looking at returns. For example, a shareholder interested in the return their company is giving may well only be concerned with profit after tax and interest. If it is performance measure that one is looking for, the profit before tax and interest is a clear indication of profit derived from using assets. Interest and taxation are related to other issues, the interest paid will depend on the financial structure of the company and the taxation dependent on the tax regime ruling at the time or in the country concerned.

As most managers will be concerned with comparing their operating performance year by year they will not want this clouded by issues such as interest or tax payments.

In the following examples return on capital employed is considered to be:

$$\frac{\text{Net operating profit (before interest and tax)}}{\text{Capital employed}}$$

This gives a clearer and more consistent method of comparing companies - so called bench-marking.

As an illustration, we will take a company which has a return on capital employed of 20%. This is the prime ratio and this ratio analysis splits up into two clear sub ratios and thus types of analysis.

$$\text{ROCE} = \frac{\textbf{Net operating profit} \text{ (before interest and tax)}}{\textbf{Capital employed}}$$

**Net profit % =**

$$\frac{\textbf{Net operating profit} \text{ (before tax and interest)}}{\textbf{Sales or turnover}}$$

$$\frac{\textbf{Sales or turnover}}{\textbf{Capital employed}} = \textbf{Asset turnover}$$

The left hand ratio is called the **net profit per cent (to sales)**.The definition of net operating profit should be the same as that used for the calculation of return on capital employed and sales is the figure of net sales or turnover in a year. The net profit per cent is the total sales less all labour, material, overhead costs. A net profit of 10% will be used as an example, although the rate of net profit will very much depend on the type of industry concerned.

The right hand ratio is called the **asset turnover ratio** or asset utilisation ratio (AUR). This is a ratio of:

$$\frac{\text{Sales or turnover (as defined in net profit\%)}}{\text{Capital employed (as defined in return on capital employed)}}$$

This ratio is expressed as a multiple, 3:1, 5:1, 10:1, rather than 300%, 500% or 1,000%. It is a measure of what sales activity (what movement of goods or services) one gets from the capital employed. Obviously, a higher multiple is seen as being more efficient but the multiple will very much depend on the type of industry being analysed. For instance, an engineering company, with high amounts of capital employed invested in plant and machinery would typically have a low multiple, 2:1 being quite common, whereas a service company, often with very little capital employed would have a high multiple, say, 4:1. Whatever the type of business, the drive will always be to produce a higher multiple as this affects the return on capital employed - the primary ratio.

Once these two subsidiary ratios have been calculated, it can be seen that the:

Net profit % x Asset turnover = Return on capital employed.

It is important to be aware of this arithmetical link. For example, if net profit per cent falls due to market place competition, one way of maintaining returns would be to become more efficient, that is, to increase sales from the capital employed used ('make the assets sweat') or reduce the capital employed.This is not surprising and is manifest in the common practice of out-sourcing or sub-contracting in business today The aim is to reduce capital employed at every turn - reduce tangible fixed assets - buildings, shops, equipment employed - and keep levels of stocks and debtors well under control.

*The sub-ratios can be analysed into groupings as follows:*

### Net profit % • gross profit % gross margin % • sales margin %

Firstly, gross profit per-cent indicates the gross profitability or margin in making and selling goods or services. This ratio will have expected values for particular types of industry. For example, a retailer might well expect a gross profit of 50%, a fast food outlet might expect a gross profit of as much as 80%. It is important to explain what gross profit is. It is the sales of a business less the cost of sales.What goes into cost of sales is up to the business concerned but there is much convention. For example, for a retailer, cost of sales should really only contain the cost of the goods being sold. For a fast food outlet, cost of sales would be the cost of the ingredients. For a manufacturer, cost of sales would be the cost of labour, materials and the overheads of a factory. Therefore, the gross profit will be quite different depending on the type of industry being reviewed.To achieve a high net profit % it is obviously important to achieve a high gross profit and the way to do this is to maximise sales margin (sell real or perceived value added products!) and keep the cost of what is being sold to a minimum.

## Overhead / expense analysis

Further ratios under net profit % are obtained from an analysis of the overhead or expense headings, for example, wages to sales; motor costs to sales; heat and light or occupancy costs to sales; telephone/fax costs to sales, etc. These ratios are used throughout industries to control the business and from a profitability point of view, they would be reviewed to try to keep the percentage as low as possible. Again, for any one business, or types of business, there will be expected ratios for these headings and it is important in any business to know what would be considered an acceptable percentage.

## Asset turnover

A further analysis of asset turnover is given by looking at turnover or sales to fixed assets; turnover or sales to stock; turnover or sales to debtors; turnover or sales or, more correctly, cost of sales to creditors.

**Turnover to fixed assets** indicates the amount of sales you get out of the value of tangible fixed assets employed. It could be more sensibly expressed, for example, for a retailer, as turnover per square metre, ie the sales value obtained from each square metre of retail space. This ratio is all about indicating efficient use of the assets. For machines use, it might be units produced per machine.

**Turnover to Stock** is a ratio of the sales compared to the stock levels, more commonly expressed as number of days of stock, in which case the ratio would be expressed as:

$$\frac{\text{Stock or turnover}}{\text{Turnover}} \text{ x 365 days (or x 52 if it should be expressed in weeks)}$$

**Note**: textbooks generally state that stock should be compared to cost of sales, as both are at cost. If margins are similar and an indicator of relative stock holdings is what is required then stock to sales is acceptable.

The principle is well known. Theoretically, a business should carry no stock but this is impractical and the aim must always be to have as little stock as possible, that is, as few days' stock as possible to meet customers needs or demands. What normal levels are will again depend on the type of business. For a supermarket, it may be that 12 days' stock is an effective and efficient minimum, whereas for a manufacturing company, minimum stock levels may have to be 60 days, due to the fact that they have to keep raw materials, they have work in progress, that is, items in the production process and they have to carry finished goods in the warehouse awaiting sale.

**Turnover to debtors** or debtors to turnover x 365 (if they are to be expressed in days) is a ratio indicating how good debt collection is. The theoretical ideal is to sell only for cash and have no debtors but this is not possible in many businesses. The aim must be to have a minimum number of days' debtors outstanding. The number of days outstanding which is normal will depend on the type of business. For example, a utility which bills at the end of a period may be able to collect all their debts within three weeks or a month as they have the threat of cutting off the supply of electricity, telephone, etc, whereas someone selling in a competitive market may have to offer extended credit and may have debtors of up to 90 days or more. The level of debt/turnover will also depend on the country and culture of the business concerned.

To gain further understanding of the calculation, meaning and use of these ratios, there follows an example which uses two different business types as the basis for analysis.

g

## Ratio analysis – review of companies M and B

| | company M | company B |
|---|---|---|
| Return on capital employed | 20.66% | 17.71% |
| Net profit % | 13.18% | 22.05% |
| Asset turnover | 1.57 | 0.80 |
| PROFITABILITY | | |
| Gross profit/margin | 35.11% | 22.05% |
| Admin costs/turnover | 21.93% | 0.00% |
| EFFICIENCY/ASSET UTILISATION | | |
| Fixed asset turnover (t/o) | 2.04 | 0.81 |
| Stock turnover (t/o) -days | 20 | 4 |
| Debtor days | 57 | 73 |
| Creditor days | 99 | 162 |

| | |
|---|---|
| ROCE | Both performing well - 15% to 20% considered to be good returns. |
| Net profit % | Good in both companies - 22% for B implies a special market or maybe it is business which needs or can command high margins. |
| Asset turnover | Adequate for M very low for B. Either B is poor at utilising assets, has inadequate sales or is a business which has a very high asset/infrastructure base. |
| Gross profit | Good for M - in fact quite high and typical of a retailer. In the published accounts from which the ratios for B were calculated the figures for gross profit and administration costs were unavailable. |
| Administration costs | Quite high administration costs for M - it depends what is included under this heading. |

| | |
|---|---|
| Fixed asset t/o | Low for both M and B - sales for the year are just twice the total assets employed for M and less than the assets employed in B. B's fixed asset turnover is typical of a utility - huge fixed asset base. |
| Stock t/o - days | Very good for both companies. 20 days stock holding is good. B is either super efficient in stock management or needs very little stock to carry on its business. |
| Debtors t/o - days | Fairly high for both companies - nearly two months for M and 2.5 months for B. |
| Creditor t/o - days | Both companies make their suppliers wait for their money! |

The companies are a high street retailer and a telecommunications company. You may now make more sense of the analysis having this information. In real life you should know in what activities the business you are reviewing is involved and also have the figures from which the ratios are calculated. These facts plus developing a knowledge of benchmark figures appropriate to the businesses which you are likely to review will mean you can get a lot out of ratio analysis. Further reviews of companies using ratio analysis may be found in Section 2.

## Checklist

- ✓ Do you know the return your business makes?
- ✓ Do you know your costs as a percentage of your sales or of total costs?
- ✓ Do you know how well your assets are utilised?
- ✓ Do you know your business?

# chapter six

## Interpretation

**Detailed ratio analysis**

**Profitability ratios**

**Asset turnover analysis**

**Stock market measures**

**Detailed performance measurement – bench marking**

**What is bench marking?**

**Checklist**

## Detailed ratio analysis

As outlined in Section 1 there are many ways of measuring the performance of a business, profitability usually being seen as the most important measure. However it is the consistent delivery of adequate and improving returns on capital employed which is the prime measure and the one which really adds shareholder value.

At various times other driving forces may dictate that other measures are seen as being the prime ones.

g

**High accounting profits** may be the prime measure where profitability is expected or has been promised(!) by the board. The word 'accounting' has been inserted to remind the reader that in spite of the relative tightness of accounting standards there may be scope to manipulate profits, certainly in the short-term.

**Sales or income growth** may be most important, obviously where market share is perceived as being most important.

**Cash flow** can be of prime importance, particularly for listed companies as there is a need to pay regular cash dividends.

The above examples may be considered as prime measures but of themselves they will not guarantee success in the long-term. Considering the primary ratio ROCE (return on capital employed) which is delivered by net profit percent times asset turnover in the example below it can be seen that a consistent return can be delivered by:

- Increasing sales whilst sacrificing percentage margin on the sales - the selling price will be lower but there will be increased volume of sales.
- Pursuing higher percentage margin but sacrificing sales volume - the selling price will be higher but sales volume will decrease.

| | Base position | Increased sales | Higher % margin |
|---|---|---|---|
| Capital employed | 300 | 300 | 300 |
| Turnover (sales) | 600 | 700 | 500 |
| Net operating profit | 60 | 60 | 60 |

**Base position**

ROCE = (Return on capital employed) $= \frac{\text{net operating profit}}{\text{capital employed}} = \frac{60}{300} = 20\%$

Net operating profit % $= \frac{\text{net operating profit}}{\text{turnover}} = \frac{60}{600} = 10\%$

Asset turnover $= \frac{\text{turnover}}{\text{capital employed}} = \frac{600}{300} = \frac{2}{1}$

**Increased sales** **lower % margin on sales/lower selling price - increased sales volume**

ROCE = (Return on capital employed) $= \frac{\text{net operating profit}}{\text{capital employed}} = \frac{60}{300} = 20\%$

Net operating profit % $= \frac{\text{net operating profit}}{\text{turnover}} = \frac{60}{700} = 9\%$

Asset turnover $= \frac{\text{turnover}}{\text{capital employed}} = \frac{700}{300} = \frac{2.3}{1}$

**Higher % margin** **higher % margin on sales/higher selling price - decreased sales volume**

ROCE = (Return on capital employed) $= \frac{\text{net operating profit}}{\text{capital employed}} = \frac{60}{300} = 20\%$

Net operating profit % $= \frac{\text{net operating profit}}{\text{turnover}} = \frac{60}{500} = 12\%$

Asset turnover $= \frac{\text{turnover}}{\text{capital employed}} = \frac{500}{300} = \frac{1.7}{1}$

In business the trick is of course to increase sales whilst increasing or at least holding margin. The following examples are developments of the base position.

**Increased sales / % margin maintained at 10%**

| | |
|---|---|
| Capital employed | 300 |
| Turnover (sales) | 700 |
| Net operating profit | 70 |

ROCE = (Return on capital employed) $= \dfrac{\text{net operating profit}}{\text{capital employed}} = \dfrac{70}{300} = 23\%$

Net operating profit % $= \dfrac{\text{net operating profit}}{\text{turnover}} = \dfrac{70}{700} = 10\%$

Asset turnover $= \dfrac{\text{turnover}}{\text{capital employed}} = \dfrac{700}{300} = \dfrac{2.3}{1}$

It is possible to improve returns with falling sales volumes, as long as margins are improved and capital employed is reduced. Capital employed should be lower with decreased levels of sales.

**Higher % margin/higher selling price - decreased sales volume but capital employed reduced**

| | |
|---|---|
| Capital employed | 250 |
| Turnover (sales) | 500 |
| Net operating profit | 60 |

ROCE = (Return on capital employed) $= \dfrac{\text{net operating profit}}{\text{capital employed}} = \dfrac{60}{250} = 24\%$

Net operating profit % $= \dfrac{\text{net operating profit}}{\text{turnover}} = \dfrac{60}{500} = 12\%$

Asset turnover $= \dfrac{\text{turnover}}{\text{capital employed}} = \dfrac{500}{250} = \dfrac{2.0}{1}$

The above examples demonstrate the need to comprehend the critical aspects of your business - which factors are most and least under your control (within acceptable time limits).

- Can margins be managed - prices increased - costs cut - quickly?
- Can margin be increased - what affect does this have on selling price?
- Can capital employed be decreased (or increased) quickly as sales volumes change?

The ratios which underlie the top three ratios contribute to getting the right outcome so a thorough understanding of them is important.

The ratios are often described as being 'a pyramid of ratios' as they spread down and out from the apex - return on capital employed.

**Return on capital employed**

**Net profit %**

$\frac{\text{expenses}}{\text{sales}}$

$\frac{\text{wages}}{\text{sales}}$ $\frac{\text{occupancy}}{\text{sales}}$ $\frac{\text{phone costs}}{\text{sales}}$

**Asset turnover**

$\frac{\text{fixed assets}}{\text{sales}}$ $\frac{\text{stock}}{\text{sales}}$ $\frac{\text{debtors}}{\text{sales}}$

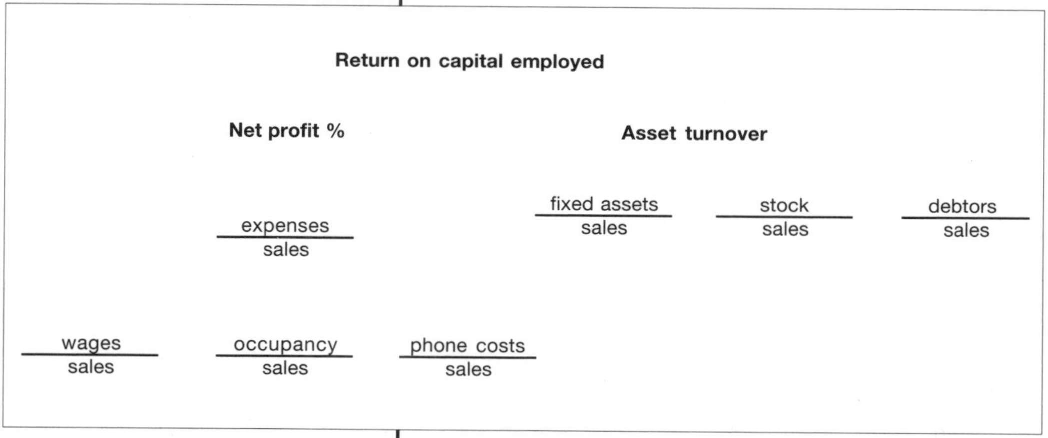

## Profitability ratios

### Gross profit %

Gross profit is the sales of a business less the cost of sales. This figure can be expressed as a percentage of the sales figure to give gross profit %. Gross profit % indicates the gross profitability or margin in making and selling goods or services. It is a very important ratio for control purposes, especially in retailing businesses.

This ratio will have expected values for particular types of industry. For example, a retailer might well expect a gross profit of 50%, a fast food outlet might expect a gross profit of as much as 80%.

What goes into cost of sales is up to the business concerned but there is much convention. For example, for a retailer, cost of sales should really only contain the cost of the goods being sold. For a fast food outlet, cost of sales would be the cost of the ingredients. For a manufacturer, cost of sales would be the cost of labour, materials and the overheads of a factory. The gross profit will be quite different depending on the type of industry being reviewed.

### Overhead or expense analysis

Further ratios may be obtained by analysing the overhead or expense headings, for example, wages to sales; motor costs to sales; heat and light or occupancy costs to sales; telephone/fax costs to sales, etc. These ratios are used throughout the business world to control businesses. From the profitability point of view, they should be reviewed to try to keep the percentage expense as low as possible. For any business there will be expected percentages for the expense headings and it is important for any business to know what are considered acceptable percentages.

### Net profit %

A high net profit % is obviously delivered by achieving as high a gross profit % as possible and keeping other expenses to a minimum.

## Asset turnover analysis

A further analysis of asset turnover is given by looking at turnover or sales to fixed assets; turnover or sales to stock; turnover or sales to debtor; turnover or sales or, more correctly, cost of sales to creditors.

### Turnover to fixed assets – fixed asset turnover ratio

This indicates the amount of sales in relation to the value of tangible fixed assets employed.This ratio indicates how assets are being utilised and whether or not they are being used efficiently.

Expressing sales to fixed asset values in currency units is not the only way of considering asset utilisation, and in any event to have reliable comparisons realistic valuations of the fixed assets would be required. For a retailer the ratio would be more sensibly expressed as turnover per square metre, ie the sales value obtained from each square metre of retail space. For a factory with machines units produced per machine would be a useful ratio.

### Turnover to stock – stock turnover

This is a ratio of the sales as a multiple of the closing stock figure. For example sales of 390,000 to year end stock of 30,000 gives the ratio 13 to 1, sales in the year are 13 times the stock held at the end of the year. Strictly speaking the ratio should be calculated using cost of sales rather than sales, as stock will be valued in the balance sheet at cost, not selling price. However, the cost of sales figure may not always be available and as long as analyses are done in a consistent manner the sales or turnover figure can be used.

This ratio is often expressed as months, weeks or days stock. For the above example a ratio of 13:1 divided into 52 weeks reveals that four weeks stock is held at the year end, assuming sales continue at a similar level.

The principle that stock levels should be as low as possible is well known. Theoretically, a business should carry no stock but this is impractical and the aim must always be to have as little stock as possible, that is, as few days' stock as possible to meet customers needs or demands.

What are acceptable levels of stock will depend on the type of business. For a supermarket, it may be that 12 days' stock is an effective and efficient minimum, whereas for a manufacturing company, minimum stock levels may have to be 60 days, due to the fact that they have to keep raw materials, they have work in progress, that is, items in the production process and they have to carry finished goods in warehouses awaiting sale.

### Turnover to debtors – debtors turnover

This is a ratio indicating how good debt collection is. Ideally you should sell only for cash and have no debtors but this is not possible in many businesses. The aim must be to have a minimum number of days' debtors outstanding. The number of days outstanding which is normal will depend on the type of business. For example, a utility which bills at the end of a period may be able to collect all their debts within three weeks or a month as they have the threat of cutting off the supply of electricity, telephone, etc, whereas someone selling in a competitive market may have to offer extended credit and may have debtors of up to 90 days or more.

## Cost of sales to creditors – creditors turnover ratio

This is a ratio indicating how promptly suppliers are paid. Strictly speaking the ratio should be calculated using cost of sales rather than sales, as creditors relate to cost or expense items. However, the cost of sales figure may not always be available and as long as analyses are done in a consistent manner the sales or turnover figure can be used. A high number of creditor days (calculated as for stock or debtor days) indicates either that the company is having difficulty in paying its suppliers or that the company is in a strong position in relation to its suppliers. The fact that some large companies are slow in paying smaller companies is a contentious issue.

Note: in the examples in this text year end figures are used for fixed assets stock debtors and creditors. It might be argued that using average figures (eg opening stock plus closing stock divided by 2) would be more accurate. This may be correct if a picture of long-term trends is required, or where it is believed year end figures may be manipulated. However from a management point of view it is the year end figures which are relevant – this is the stock that exists, there never was an amount of 'average' stock in existence!

## Ratio analysis example

Set out below are summarised profit and loss accounts and balance sheets for three companies M, S and T plc. These three companies have been chosen as they are in the same business sector and the analysis will demonstrate basic inter company comparison through the use of ratios. Furthermore, the business sector has been chosen as it is one with which most of us are familiar - we've been there either willingly otherwise!

A logical approach is to group the ratios as follows:

**Stage I: calculate the primary ratios:**

Return on Capital Employed $= \dfrac{\text{Net Operating Profit}}{\text{Capital Employed}}$

Net Profit % $= \dfrac{\text{Net Operating Profit}}{\text{Turnover or Sales}}$

Asset Turnover $= \dfrac{\text{Turnover or Sales}}{\text{Capital Employed}}$

**Stage II: calculate profitability related ratios:**

Gross Profit % $= \dfrac{\text{Gross Profit}}{\text{Turnover}}$

Administration Costs/Turnover= $\dfrac{\text{Administration Costs}}{}$

Net Profit % $= \dfrac{\text{Net Operating Profit}}{\text{Turnover or Sales}}$

**Stage III: calculate ratios concerned with efficiency – asset utilisation:**

Fixed Asset Turnover = $\frac{\text{Turnover}}{\text{Tangible Fixed Assets}}$

Stock Turnover (Days) = $\frac{\text{WIP and Stock (x 365)}}{\text{Turnover}}$

Debtor Days = $\frac{\text{Debtors (x 365)}}{\text{Turnover}}$

Creditor Days = $\frac{\text{Creditors (x 365)}}{\text{Cost of Sales}}$

**Stage IV: calculate liquidity and gearing ratios (Chapter 2 – Section 2):**

Current Ratio = $\frac{\text{Current Assets}}{\text{Current Liabilities}}$

Liquidity Ratio or Acid Test = $\frac{\text{Current Assets less Stocks}}{\text{Current Liabilities}}$

Gearing Ratio = $\frac{\text{long-term Liabilities or Loans}}{\text{Capital Employed}}$

The figures have been extracted from the 2xx7 accounts of the three companies and for simplification, creditors have not been analysed in any detail, that is between overdraft or current portions of loans repayable or trade and other creditors.

| **P & L account extracts** | | M | S | T |
|---|---|---|---|---|
| Turnover | A | 7,842 | 13,395 | 13,887 |
| Cost of Sales | B | 5,104 | 12,413 | 12,846 |
| Gross Profit | C | 2,738 | 982 | 1,041 |
| Administration Costs | D | 1,700 | 287 | 267 |
| Net Operating Profit | E | 1,038 | 695 | 774 |
| **Balance sheet extracts** | | | | |
| Fixed Assets | F | 3,647 | 6,041 | 5,849 |
| Current Assets | | | | |
| stock | G | 445 | 744 | 550 |
| debtors | H | 1,726 | 253 | 78 |
| bank/cash | I | 1,033 | 248 | 145 |
| total | J | 3,204 | 1,245 | 773 |
| Current Liabilities | | | | |
| overdraft | K | 0 | 0 | 0 |
| creditors | L | 1,775 | 2,804 | 2,101 |
| total | M | 1,775 | 2,804 | 2,101 |
| Working Capital | N | 1,429 | -1,559 | -1,328 |
| **Total assets - current liabilities** | **O** | **5,076** | **4,482** | **4,521** |
| Long Term Liabilities | P | -528 | -811 | -631 |
| | Q | 4,548 | 3,671 | 3,890 |
| Shareholders' funds | | | | |
| Share Capital | R | 709 | 460 | 109 |
| p & l account | S | 3,104 | 2,081 | 2,310 |
| other | T | 735 | 1,130 | 1,471 |
| | U | 4,548 | 3,671 | 3,890 |
| **CAPITAL EMPLOYED = U+P =** | **V** | **5,076** | **4,482** | **4,521** |
| **I Principal ratios** | | | | |
| Return on capital employed | E/V | 20.45% | 15.51% | 17.12% |
| Net profit % | E/A | 13.24% | 5.19% | 5.57% |
| Asset turnover | A/V | 1.54 | 2.99 | 3.07 |
| **II Profitability** | | | | |
| Gross Profit/Margin | C/A | 34.91% | 7.33% | 7.50% |
| Admin Costs/Turnover | D/A | 21.68% | 2.14% | 1.92% |
| Net Profit % | E/A | 13.24% | 5.19% | 5.57% |
| **III Efficiency/asset utilisation** | | | | |
| Fixed Asset Turnover | A/F | 2.15 | 2.22 | 2.37 |
| Stock Turnover(days) | G/Ax365 | 21 | 20 | 14 |
| Debtor days | H/Ax365 | 80 | 7 | 2 |
| Creditor days | L/Bx365 | 127 | 82 | 60 |
| **IV Liquidity and gearing ratios** | | | | |
| Current Ratio | J/M | 1.81 | 0.44 | 0.37 |
| Liquidity Ratio | (J-G)/M | 1.55 | 0.18 | 0.11 |
| Gearing Ratio | P/V | 10.40% | 18.09% | 13.96% |

**Company M**

***I***

| | |
|---|---|
| Good return<br>Very good net profit<br>Asset turnover on the low side | A 'benchmark' company |

***II***

| | |
|---|---|
| High GP | A retailer? |
| Reasonable administration costs | |

***III***

| | |
|---|---|
| Fixed asset turnover not high | Poor use of assets or high property value – a retailer with prime sites? |
| Stock turnover excellent | Short shelf-life products?<br>A retailer |
| Debtor days high | Extended credit giver? |
| Creditor days > debtor days | Good working capital management |

***IV***

Cash well managed

Low gearing

**Company S**

***I***

| | |
|---|---|
| Reasonable return | Reasonable performance |
| Low net profit | |
| Good asset turnover | |

***II***

| | |
|---|---|
| Low GP | How is GP calculated? |
| Low administration costs | Competitive market |
| | Are these included in Cost of Sales? |

***III***

| | |
|---|---|
| Fixed asset turnover not high | High assets values – new assets |
| Stock turnover excellent | Very short shelf-life products |
| Debtor days very low | Selling for cash? – a retailer |
| Creditor days > Debtor days | Good working capital management |

***IV***

Cash well managed

Low gearing

**Company T**

***I***

| | |
|---|---|
| Good return<br>Low net profit<br>Asset turnover good | Competitive market?<br>Good sales volumes? |

***II***

| | |
|---|---|
| Low GP | How is GP calculated? |
| Low administration costs | Competitive market<br>Are these included in cost of sales |

***III***

| | |
|---|---|
| Fixed asset turnover higher than M or S | Better use of assets<br>Higher sales volume – cheaper sites? |
| Stock turnover excellent | Short shelf-life products |
| Debtor days very low | Selling for cash? – a retailer |
| Creditor days > Debtor days | Good working capital management |

***IV***

Cash well managed

Gearing low

It is undoubtedly easier to make the above comments with knowledge of the companies and their current performance, but even the basic ratios above can tell much about a company's performance.

In the examples analysing M, S and T the balance sheet extracts show the most common UK layout of balance sheets referenced so that the capital employed may be found.

Basically capital employed can be considered as the fixed assets and working capital employed in the business and this should of course exactly equal the shareholders' equity and the creditors: amounts falling due after more than one year.

There may have to be investigation as to whether or not continuing overdrafts are not in fact 'core' borrowing and whether or not provisions and charges, although classed as long term liabilities, should really be excluded as sources of funding.

## US balance sheets – the figure for capital employed

The balance sheet of the oil corporation in Chapter 1, Section 2 can be rearranged as follows to reveal the capital employed.

| | | |
|---|---|---|
| total current assets | | 17,318 |
| investments and advances | | 5,697 |
| property, plant and equipment | | 65,446 |
| other assets | | 2,835 |
| total assets | | 91,296 |
| less current liabilities | | 18,736 |
| **capital employed** | | **72,560** |
| shareholders' equity | | 40,436 |
| long term liabilities | | |
| long term debt | | 7,778 |
| annuity reserves | | 8,770 |
| deferred income | | 12,431 |
| deferred credits | | 975 |
| equity of minority | | 2,170 |
| **capital employed/invested** | | **72,560** |

## Stock market measures

Another area of performance measurement is that of measuring the performance of a company by its performance in relation to other listed or quoted companies - how does it perform in relation to the market?

The following terms and ratios are the principal ones used when considering stock market performance.

### Share values

There are three shares values commonly quoted and they are as follows:

- Nominal (par) value
- Book (asset) value
- Market value

*Nominal (par) value*

The nominal value is the value of the ordinary shares or stock eg 1,000,000 25p shares nominal value is 250,000.

*Book value*

This value is arrived at by dividing the number of issued shares into the shareholders' funds.

*Market value*

This is the price quoted in the Stock Exchange for a public company or an estimated price for a non-quoted company. On the Stock Exchange the figure changes daily in response to actual or anticipated results and overall sentiment of the market.

### Earnings per share (EPS)

Earnings per share is one of the most widely quoted performance measures when there is a discussion of a company's performance or share value.

The profit used in the calculation is the profit available to shareholders after all other claimants have been satisfied. The most common prior charges in the profit and loss account are interest and tax.

The profit is divided by the number of issued shares to calculate the value of earnings per share. This figure tells us what profit has been earned by the shareholder for every share held. There is an accounting standard which further defines profit and number of shares as it may be possible to manipulate these figures.

One important piece of additional information is that the 'fully diluted' EPS should be shown. Fully diluted means that if all options on shares, to directors, employees or to those holders of loans which can be converted into ordinary shares were taken up then obviously the number of shares in existence would increase and the EPS figure would fall. A much lower fully diluted EPS figure indicates many options in existence or a high level of convertible loans.

### Dividends per share (DPS)

Normally only a proportion of the profit available to the shareholders is paid out to them in cash, the remainder being retained to allow the business to grow.

The proportion paid out will depend on many factors, but a reasonable proportion for a successful business which has growth potential would be 30% to 50% of the available profits. As dividends amount and dividend growth is seen as of great importance by analysts and shareholders companies will want to pay sufficient dividends to satisfy them. Companies dislike intensely to have to reduce dividends because this will drive away investors with possibly serious effects on share price. A company in a difficult year will often decide that it must pay a dividend in excess of the current year's available profit rather than cut the dividend. This is done by paying dividends out of past years' retained profits.

## Dividend cover

This is a ratio of profits available for ordinary shareholders expressed as a multiple of the total dividends paid and payable. It can also be found by dividing EPS by DPS.

Companies adopt dividend policies to suit their business needs. These will reflect the sectors in which they operate and the specific strategies they adopt.

- A high cover suggests that the dividend is fairly safe, because it can be maintained in the face of any expected downturn in profit.
- A high cover also indicates a high retention policy, which suggests that the company is aiming for growth.

## Earnings yield and dividend yield

The yield on a share can be expressed as the return it provides in terms of earnings or dividends as a percentage of the current share price.

The earnings yield shows the relationship that EPS bears to the share price. For instance, if the EPS is 1.50 and the share price is 10.00% the earnings yield is 15%. If the share price moved up to 15.00% the corresponding yield would be 10%. A low yield generally indicates a share that is in demand from investors.

## Price to earnings ratio (PE ratio)

The price to earnings ratio is a widely quoted measure of share value. The share price is divided by the EPS figure.

A company has no direct control over the PE ratio. In the long-term, however, it must deliver a good return to the equity shareholder to secure a continued high rating.

The advantages of a high price to earnings ratio value are considerable. New funds can be raised at a favourable price.

The company has the means to make acquisitions on favourable terms by using its 'paper' (shares), as opposed to cash.

### Market to book ratio

The ratio relates the total market capitalisation of the company to the shareholders' funds.

It is the investors' perception of the performance of the company in terms of profits, balance sheet strength or liquidity and growth that determines this ratio.

A value of less that one means that the shareholders' investment has diminished in value.

### Operating Profit

This should be the profit from the continuing 'normal' business activities, e.g. it would exclude rental income, if any.

### EBIT

Earnings before interest and tax.

This should be the profit of the business from all sources and after any exceptional expense (or income). BUT businesses and analysts will sometimes leave items (costs) out, on the basis that they are 'one-off' – the aim is to reveal 'underlying' earnings.

### EBITDA

Earnings before interest, tax depreciation and amortisation

All the rage – quite why? The only explanation is that at least this figure of 'Profitability' is not distorted by accounting slight of hand! It is really a figure of gross cash generation.

## Detailed performance measurement – bench marking

Much is made of performance measurement and bench marking and everyone appears to know about the topics and what to do! There are very many sources of data which permit comparison of performance and thus companies can determine how they operate with respect to the best. Comparison of performance will be to no avail if action is not taken to emulate the best. Taking action is no mere accounting exercise, but requires management, team work maybe, but most of all leadership.

## What is bench marking?

For any business there will be facts, numbers and ratios which indicate the performance of the business. The key is to identify the data for the apparently best performer. The word 'apparent' has been used, as care must be taken when choosing the bench mark company:

- Is it as good as it claims?
- Is it really appropriate to use it as a comparative?
- Are the data used by the company being compared reliable and compiled on the same basis as the best?

Performance measurement is then comparing a company's performance with the best. To be of any use there must then be **ACTION.**

Bench marking is the process of learning from the best to become and stay the best. This is done by the measuring of business performance against the best with constant effort in continuously reviewing the business processes, practices and methods. It is important to consider exactly why you wish to bench mark – what drives bench marking? Is it because:

- it's the done thing!
- of global competition
- quality systems and certification
- a desire to improve and be the best.

The last reason would seem to be the best, but the others may be valid. Ratio analysis described in this section is an important part of a bench marking process, but the list below makes the point that true bench marking has to be a structured process, with ratio analysis and performance measurement being an important part.

### Bench marking should be a structured process

- Learn from others
- Adapt to your own business
- Take action - try to exceed the best.

*Implement properly:*

- The existing business process must be understood
- Bench marking must be an integral part of business strategy
- Bench marking must be planned, organised and implemented
- Bench marking should be driven and adopted by all
- Bench marking must be taken seriously.

## Ratio analysis – question

Calculate the three principle ratios for the hotel chain studied earlier.

## Ratio analysis – feedback

From the hotels chain s accounts shown previously the 2xx5 figures are as follows:

| | | £m | |
|---|---|---|---|
| P&L account | | | |
| turnover | a | 1,789 | |
| net operating profit | b | 258 | |
| balance sheet | | | |
| fixed assets | c | 4,032 | |
| stock | d | 47 | |
| debtors | e | 232 | |
| creditors | f | 480 | |
| capital employed | g | 4,041 | this is total assets less current liabilities or also total equity (h) plus creditors due after one year (i) |

return on capital employed=

$$\textbf{ROCE} = \frac{\text{net operating profit}}{\text{capital employed}} = \frac{258}{4{,}041} = \textbf{6.4\%}$$

$$\text{net profit \%} = \frac{\text{net operating profit}}{\text{turnover}} = \frac{258}{1{,}789} = \textbf{14.4\%}$$

$$\text{asset turover} = \frac{\text{turnover}}{\text{capital employed}} = \frac{1{,}789}{4{,}041} = \textbf{0.44} \text{ times}$$

On the face of it the above ratios indicate poor performance.

The return of 6.4% is very low compared with other businesses. The actual return in the form of dividends to share price at any time may of course be quite different. However, the fact remains that the capital employed is not being made to deliver results.

The net profit percent appears quite high, but this is an industry which should have gross margins of 60+ per cent on food and liquor sales.

The asset turnover is poor, this is a result of the capital employed being in the form of (expensive) property and also the fact that the assets are under utilised - sales could be higher.

The company was taken over in the year following and from just these three ratios the actions to take to improve performance are obvious.

- Cut capital employed - under performing properties
- Increase sales revenues
- Cut costs and improve margins.

## Checklist

- ✓ Understand your business through figures and ratios.
- ✓ Have a knowledge of the best performers in your business sector.
- ✓ Question why your ratios are not better.

# chapter seven

section one

## Cash budgeting

Cash flow forecasts

Outline of a simple cash flow forecast

Checklist

## Cash flow forecasts

Cash flow forecasts are often the simplest financial statements to produce - they simply contain projections of cash flows - inflows from sales or investment and outflows due to cash payments for fixed asset purchase, operating costs or finance costs (interest and loan repayments).

### The need for a cash flow forecast

Whether for a new business venture or continuation of an existing business, managers must be aware of the expected cash balance or requirement over the life of the business or project. If you run out of cash you go bust!

Cash flow forecasts require some basic budgeting skills - you need to know what your objective is, what your income/costs will be and when they will occur.

A very simple cash flow forecast is set out below:

| Cash Flow Forecast | | | for the 6 months ending... | | | | |
|---|---|---|---|---|---|---|---|
| | Jan | Feb | Mar | Apr | May | Jun | Total |
| **Inflows** | | | | | | | |
| Sales | 500 | 2000 | 3000 | 5000 | 5000 | 5000 | |
| Sundry | | | | | | | |
| Capital | 20000 | | | | | | |
| | **20500** | **2000** | **3000** | **5000** | **5000** | **5000** | **40500** |
| **Outflows** | | | | | | | |
| Cost of sales | 250 | 1000 | 1500 | 2500 | 2500 | 2500 | |
| Wages | 400 | 400 | 400 | 400 | 400 | 400 | |
| Rent | 100 | 100 | 100 | 100 | 100 | 100 | |
| Fuel | 50 | 50 | 50 | 50 | 50 | 50 | |
| Insurance | 40 | 40 | 40 | 40 | 40 | 40 | |
| Fixed assets | 19500 | | | | | | |
| Loan repayments | | 600 | 600 | 600 | 600 | 600 | |
| | **20340** | **2190** | **2690** | **3690** | **3690** | **3690** | **36290** |
| | | | | | | | |
| **Net Cash Flow** | 160 | -190 | 310 | 1310 | 1310 | 1310 | 4210 |
| Brought forward | 0 | 160 | -30 | 280 | 1590 | 2900 | |
| | | | | | | | |
| **Carried forward** | **160** | **-30** | **280** | **1590** | **2900** | **4210** | |

A prime aim of cash management, whether in the short or long-term, is to remain within the business's set cash parameters. For many businesses this means having a positive amount as a cash or bank balance at the end of any day or remaining within the maximum overdraft limit each day.

As an aid to understanding a business's cash position and cash requirements, it is essential to track and budget the cash flows in and out of the business. A cash flow forecast is the tool which enables a business's cash requirements to be modelled. The aim is to identify cash requirements over the period being studied, particularly the maximum requirement for funding - the required overdraft limit. Hopefully businesses generate cash and therefore it is important to know the amount and timing of cash surpluses generated. This enables managers to plan payments to funders - dividends to shareholders, loan and interest payments to banks and investment in fixed assets.

g

## Layout of cash flow forecasts and cash flow modelling

The exact amount of detail and layout of a business's cash flows will depend on the company's business and the preferences of the preparer. However, the essential layout and features are set out below.

### Cash flow forecasts

**Inflows** - by type if appropriate

**Outflows** - by type as appropriate. It is better to group outflows by type, particularly distinguishing between capital (fixed asset), operating and financial (loan repayment and interest payment) cash flows.

**Net flow for the period**

**Cumulative cash flow at period end**

If the cash flow is prepared on a spreadsheet, it is sensible to build in as much flexibility as is necessary, that is, the more uncertain and material (large) figures should be input in a separate input area where figures can more easily be changed.

**Input area**

| | Jan | Feb | Mar | April |
|---|---|---|---|---|
| **Sales** | 2,000 | 3,000 | 4,000 | 4,000 |
| sales margin | | 50% | | |
| increase/decrease in sales | | 0% | | |

**Cash flow forecast for the year ending...**

| | | | | | |
|---|---|---|---|---|---|
| **Inflows** | | | | | |
| | Sales | 2,000 | 3,000 | 4,000 | 4,000 |
| **Outflows** | | | | | |
| | Materials | 1,000 | 1,500 | 2,000 | 2,000 |

***with a 40 % margin, but sales 10% higher***

**Input area**

| | Jan | Feb | Mar | April |
|---|---|---|---|---|
| **Sales** | 2,000 | 3,000 | 4,000 | 4,000 |
| sales margin | | 40% | | |
| increase/decrease in sales | | 10% | | |

**Cash flow forecast for the year ending...**

| | | | | | |
|---|---|---|---|---|---|
| **Inflows** | | | | | |
| | Sales | 2,200 | 3,300 | 4,400 | 4,400 |
| **Outflows** | | | | | |
| | Materials | 1,320 | 1,980 | 2,640 | 2,640 |

With an input area and appropriate referencing of the cell content it is very easy to amend the content of the cashflow forecast. For example the opposite example could be changed:

The cell referencing used above is as follows:

| | A | B | C |
|---|---|---|---|
| 1 | | | |
| 2 | | | |
| 3 | **Input area** | | |
| 4 | | Jan | Feb |
| 5 | **Sales** | 2000 | 3000 |
| 6 | | | |
| 7 | sales margin | | 0.4 |
| 8 | increase/decrease in sales | | 0.1 |
| 9 | | | |
| 10 | | | |
| 11 | | | |
| 12 | **Cash flow forecast** | | |
| 13 | | | |
| 14 | **Inflows** | | |
| 15 | Sales | =B$5*(1+$C$8) | =C$5*(1+$C$8) |
| 16 | | | |
| 17 | **Outflows** | | |
| 18 | Materials | =B15*(1-$C$7) | =C15*(1-$C$7) |
| 19 | | | |

Basic sales data is entered in B5, C5 etc. C7 contains the margin % which can be altered as required. The possible % changes in the expected sales (in B5, C5 etc) is entered in C8.

The formula for sales is then expected sales times 1+ % change = B$5*(1+$C$8), the $ sign simply locking the cell reference to simplify replication of the formula through the required range.

The formula for materials cost is then the sales figure times 1 - the margin % = B15*(1-$c$7).

A cashflow forecast can of course simply be rows and columns of figures, but the use of simple formulae as above permits quite comprehensive sensitivity analysis to be carried out.

The preparation of a spreadsheet with forecast figures is essential but equally a cash flow forecast which will be presented to a bank or the providers of finance must set out the objective of the business or project for which the cash is required and, most importantly of all, set out the sources of data from which the cash flow forecast is prepared and state any assumptions made.

Set out on the following pages is the outline of a simple cash flow forecast starting with the most important objectives, background, bases and assumptions.

## Outline of a simple cash flow forecast

### Toy trading company

***Cash flow forecast for the first year of business to 31 December 1998***

### Outline and objectives of the business

The business will be a specialised retailer of small electronic toys.

The owners believe that the market for such products is at present not well served and there is every prospect of good sales now and in the future. Data on import and sales volume of such toys can be found in appendix A (not shown here).

The owners intend to invest 40,000 of their own funds to cover start up costs and as working capital - initial stock. After the first year of operation they expect to make a return on this investment of at least 15% after drawing reasonable salaries for the time they spend running and managing the business.

## Business structure and details

The business will operate as a partnership from premises leased at ______________________________

The partners are: names and addresses ______________

______________________________________________

______________________________________________

Possibly bank, accountants, lawyers names ___________

______________________________________________

## Basis of data and assumptions

The following sources and basis have been used, any assumptions being clearly noted.

### Sales

Sales are based on market research on existing total UK sales of such products, pro rated to the local area. An increase in base sales of 12% has been made as the consumer profile for the shop's customers indicates more higher spending individuals than the UK average. The data supporting this is given in appendix A (not shown here).

### Cost of sales

The cost of sales is based on achieving a gross margin of 55%. This margin is regularly achieved by both large and small retailers selling such products. See appendix B (not shown here) then,

### Wages, occupancy costs etc.

### Summary

A very brief commentary describing the key figures from the most likely cash flow forecast outcome. For example, the growing sales, relatively fixed outflows and the increasing cumulative cash balance.

### Cash flow forecast print outs

One or more print outs will be attached.

The best estimate or most likely outcome should be shown first. The key figures thereon could be discussed with for example the relationship of growing sales, with costs and thus outflows remaining relatively fixed in amount and thus the increasing cumulative cash balance.

The above is just an outline and a cash flow forecast could be much more detailed. It is however important to be as factual as possible, using as reliable data as possible to substantiate the figures. Flowery description may help sell the cash flow forecast to some, but it is prudent reliable figures which are wanted, particularly for inflows.

## Checklist

- ✓ A cash flow is more than numbers.
- ✓ Objectives of the forecast business proposal should be stated.
- ✓ Assumptions should be clearly stated.
- ✓ Sources of data should be given.
- ✓ Sensitive and risk areas should be identified.

# chapter seven

section two

## Cash budgeting

What is capital expenditure?

Cash flow forecasts

Non-discounted measures

Discounted cash flow techniques and measures

Sensitivity analysis

Checklist

## What is capital expenditure?

Capital expenditure usually refers to expenditure of relatively large sums of money on long-term assets, typical examples are:

- Replacement of worn out assets with new ones.
- Development of new business opportunities.

Investment inevitably means the expenditure of cash and thus it is essential to budget and appraise this expenditure.

The essential criteria for any investment is that it should make a good or at least adequate return. This will be achieved through maximising income, minimising costs, maximising the use of the investment - maximising sales, production and the volume of business carried out with the assets. Finally the investment (in capital to be employed) should be kept to a minimum - investing only that capital which is necessary to achieve the desired output. Capital expenditure has also to be incurred to comply with safety and environmental regulations.

The challenge is to evaluate the benefits, worth or the projected return on the capital expenditure before committing expenditure. Budgeting capital expenditure is much wider than simply deciding what tangible fixed assets, plant and equipment should be purchased.

The word 'project' may be over used today, but it is sensible to think of the activities into which a company enters as being in the form of projects - discrete new ventures. Past events of a company may be presented in financial statements in many ways, but future events are most clearly seen as series of cash flows in and out of the business. The concepts and arithmetic of appraising the future cash flows of capital expenditure or projects can be employed to demonstrate the viability of investment.

This section outlines the basic arithmetic used in appraisals, reviews the need for sound cash flow forecasts, indicates how models may be prepared, the measures which can be used and finally outlines a consistent and integrated process for budgeting capital expenditure or projects.

## Basic arithmetic of appraisal

### *Introduction*

The worth, value or cost of a project depends on two variables:

- The actual amounts of cash received or paid, and
- The timing of the receipts or payments.

Appraisal involves estimating both the future cash flows and the timing of the cash flows.This is the difficult part of capital expenditure budgeting or project appraisal, the arithmetic is simple.

### *Time value of money*

The timing of receipts or payments is important because an amount of money received today is worth more than the same amount received later in time.

If you were offered 1,000 now or 1,000 in one year's time you would obviously take the money today. However, what if you were offered 1,000 today or 1,800 in one year's time which would you chose? Firstly there is a cost of money, the so called time value of money. Money never comes free - it is a commodity (really a means of trading in other commodities) and thus in managed economies has an appropriate scarcity value. If there were no inflation in economies the 'real' cost of money, the real interest rate might be 4 or 5%. For practical business purposes the rate required will be the bank borrowing rate as an absolute minimum or more likely the opportunity cost of money - equal or greater than cost of capital of the company. In simple terms the cost of capital of a business is the weighted average of the rate of return required by shareholders and lenders.

For the remainder of this section we shall use typical UK or US required rates of 12 to 20%.

Returning to the above example, if you could invest the 1,000 today to give a rate of return of say 15% then it would be worth while to wait for the 1,800. The 1,000 today would only be worth 1,500 in a year's time at the 15% rate of return. However, there is also the question of risk and it might be better to accept the 1,000 today rather than hold out for the 1,800 - a bird in the hand - ! The concept of early certainty of cash flows in and out underlies a well known point on the importance of managing project and loan risk - get the money back quickly!

### Compounding and discounting

The time value of money is accounted for by the simple concept of compounding interest.

There is a rate required, this can be the interest rate on a loan, the cost of capital of the company. If the calculations are concerned with discounting then strictly speaking the term discount rate should be used: the point is that there is a time value or rate for money, whatever it may be called.

Compounded amounts increase in a geometrical progression. At the the end of a period - normally a year, 1 becomes 1 + the interest rate. With a rate of 12% 1 becomes = 1.12. This is then the base sum on which interest is calculated for the second year. The sum at the end of the second year = 1.12 x 1.12 = 1.2544 and so on.

Discounted future amounts are decreased by a similar progression. Discounting is the inverse of compounding.

The table below shows the progression in compounding or discounting over five years.

rate = 12% for one currency unit:-

| Year | **compounded amount** (future amount, worth or value) | **discounted amount** (present amount, worth or value) |
|---|---|---|
| 0 | 1.000 | 1.000 |
| 1 | 1.120 | 0.893 |
| 2 | 1.254 | 0.797 |
| 3 | 1.405 | 0.712 |
| 4 | 1.574 | 0.636 |
| 5 | 1.762 | 0.567 |

Tables of compound and discount factors exist, but it is easier to obtain the factors from a spreadsheet calculation as above. These factors form an integral part of an appraisal model. The formulae and notation are as follows:

## Notation and formulae

| | |
|---|---|
| Required/interest/discount rate | r or i |
| Number of years or periods | y or n |
| Future amount, worth or value | F |
| Present amount, worth or value | P |

**The compound factor = $(1+r)^{\wedge n}$**

^ is the symbol for 'to the power', upper case on the key for 6 on the keyboard.

**The discount factor = $1/(1+r)^{\wedge n}$ or $(1+r)^{\wedge n}$**

In the spreadsheet below the formulae are 'locked' with the $ signs to the year column and the interest rate cell. This means that when entered in one appropriate cell the formulae may just be copied down to give the years' factors.

| | A | B | C | D | E |
|---|---|---|---|---|---|
| 1 | rate = | 0.12 | | | |
| 2 | | | | | |
| 3 | | | **compounded amount** | | **discounted amount** |
| 4 | | | | | |
| 5 | Year | | | | |
| 6 | 0 | | =(1+$B$1)^$A6 | | =(1+$B$1)^-$A6 |
| 7 | 1 | | =(1+$B$1)^$A7 | | =(1+$B$1)^-$A7 |
| 8 | 2 | | =(1+$B$1)^$A8 | | =(1+$B$1)^-$A8 |
| 9 | 3 | | =(1+$B$1)^$A9 | | =(1+$B$1)^-$A9 |
| 10 | 4 | | =(1+$B$1)^$A10 | | =(1+$B$1)^-$A10 |
| 11 | 5 | | =(1+$B$1)^$A11 | | =(1+$B$1)^-$A11 |
| 12 | | | | | |
| 13 | | | | | |

## Cash flow forecasts

Assembling of figures of cash flows in and out is essential but equally essential a cash flow forecast which is to be used as a basis of appraisal must set out the following:

- The reasons or business objectives for the capital expenditure
- The sources of data from which the cash flow forecast is prepared
- A statement of any assumptions made.

The fact that it is future cash flows out and in which are to be appraised means that there should be no difficulties with cost definitions, however, common errors which are made are as follows:

- **Depreciation** costs are included. This is quite wrong as these costs are not cash costs and in any event if depreciation was included there would be double counting. The cash flow relating to the asset is the cash expenditure on the asset at the time of purchase. Depreciation is the accounting exercise of spreading or matching the cost of the asset over its useful working life.

- **Interest and loan repayments** are included. Again this is quite wrong as the exercise of discounting the cash flows over the life of the asset or project at the required rate takes account of the cost of money and will indicate whether or nor sufficient funds will be generated to cover loan interest and capital repayments.

- **Sunk and opportunity costs**. It is often the case that if a project is sanctioned then there will have been costs incurred in the past which benefit the project now being considered.These are sunk costs and have no relevance to the appraisal.Also the sanctioning of a project may give rise to a loss of income or costs to be incurred elsewhere - these costs may be relevant. The simple test to challenge anyone who wants to bring in sunk or opportunity costs is to ask the question 'do we have to spend cash or are we denying ourselves cash as a result of proceeding with this project?'

There are many appraisal measures - **NONE** of which tell us whether to invest or not - they can only indicate whether or not investment may be acceptable within the assumed parameters. Later the sensitivity of parameters and the risk of not achieving the desired outcome or return is considered. Firstly non-discounted and discounted methods which are commonly used are reviewed.

## Non-discounted measures

### Accounting rate of return (ROCE/ROI/RONA)

This is the calculation of the year by year accounting profit of a business earned on the investment - the historical return on capital employed or invested. It is thus a measure of past performance for one year.

It is not an acceptable appraisal measure for the following reasons, it only assesses one year's activities and assumes that all years' profits and capital employed are similar. It does not take account of the time value of money.

### Payback period

This is the calculation of the time taken to recover the initial investment. It would be calculated as follows for the sample cash flows given below:

| | cash out | cashflows:- cash in | net cash flow | cumulative non-discounted cash flow | |
|---|---|---|---|---|---|
| Year | | | | | |
| 0 | -9,000 | | -9,000 | -9,000 | |
| 1 | | 1,000 | 1,000 | -8,000 | |
| 2 | | 3,000 | 3,000 | -5,000 | |
| 3 | | 5,000 | 5,000 | **0** | **payback year** |
| 4 | | 5,000 | 5,000 | 5,000 | |
| 5 | | 4,000 | 4,000 | 9,000 | |

Whilst this is easy to calculate and comprehend it is too simplistic a measure. It takes no account of the time value of money and more significantly does not take account of cash flows after the date of payback - it therefore discriminates against longer term projects. It may be of help where risk has to be avoided and may also be of use when ranking alternatives.

## Discounted cash flow techniques and measures

Both accounting rate of return and payback are too simplistic in approach and a fundamental weakness in both methods is the fact that they ignore the effect of the timing of investment outflows and related inflows.

### Net Present Value (NPV) or Present Worth

This is defined as the present value of discounted inflows less discounted outflows.

If the NPV > 0 at the required interest rate then the project may be accepted.

If the NPV < 0 at the required interest rate then the project should be rejected.

Using the same sample figures as for the calculation of payback the NPV can be calculated as follows:

| rate = 12% | | | | | | |
|---|---|---|---|---|---|---|
| | | | cashflows: | | | |
| | discount factor | cash out | cash in | net cash flow | | discounted cash flows |
| | a | b | c | d | | e = a x d |
| Year | | | | | | |
| 0 | 1.000 | -9,000 | | -9,000 | | -9,000 |
| 1 | 0.893 | | 1,000 | 1,000 | | 893 |
| 2 | 0.797 | | 3,000 | 3,000 | | 2,392 |
| 3 | 0.712 | | 5,000 | 5,000 | | 3,559 |
| 4 | 0.636 | | 5,000 | 5,000 | | 3,178 |
| 5 | 0.567 | | 4,000 | 4,000 | | 2,270 |
| | | | net present amount or value - NPV = (the sum of column e) | | | **3,291** |

## Internal Rate of Return (IRR) or DCF yield

The internal rate of return is calculated as being the rate at which the NPV of a project is zero. This is found by trial and error.

If the IRR > the required rate then the project may be accepted.

If the IRR < the required rate then the project should be rejected.

Again, using the same sample data as for payback and NPV the IRR can be found by increasing the required rate to 23.38% at which rate the NPV is exactly zero. A higher required or discount rate would cause the NPV to be negative.

| rate = | **23.38%** | = | **the internal rate of return - IRR** | | |
|---|---|---|---|---|---|
| | | | cashflows: | | |
| | discount factor | cash out | cash in | net cash flow | discounted cash flows |
| | a | b | c | d | e = a x d |
| Year | | | | | |
| 0 | 1.000 | -9,000 | | -9,000 | -9,000 |
| 1 | 0.811 | | 1,000 | 1,000 | 811 |
| 2 | 0.657 | | 3,000 | 3,000 | 1,971 |
| 3 | 0.532 | | 5,000 | 5,000 | 2,662 |
| 4 | 0.432 | | 5,000 | 5,000 | 2,158 |
| 5 | 0.350 | | 4,000 | 4,000 | 1,399 |
| | | | net present amount or value - NPV = (the sum of column e) | | **0** |

## Sensitivity analysis

Sensitivity analysis means measuring the sensitivity of the parameters in the basic model. This requires a 'most likely case' - neither optimistic or pessimistic, base model of the project. The simple but effective approach of carrying out a 'one at a time' sensitivity analysis may then be adopted.

## 'One at a time' approach

This method looks at changes in all or at least those considered the most critical (sensitive) parameters one at a time, eg if selling price is considered the most critical parameter what decrease from the expected sales can be tolerated before the project is not viable – that is NPV is down to zero.

Again, using the basic model, but with more detail showing sales inflows and operating outflows rather than just the net inflows, a sensitivity analysis of the model may be carried out.

| rate =12% | | | | | | | |
|---|---|---|---|---|---|---|---|
| | | | cashflows: | | | | |
| | discount factor | cash out | cash in | cash out | net cash flow | | discounted cash flows |
| Year | | | | | | | |
| 0 | 1 | -9,000 | | | -9,000 | .000 | -9,000 |
| 1 | 0 | | 2,000 | -1,000 | 1,000 | .893 | 893 |
| 2 | 0 | | 6,000 | -3,000 | 3,000 | .797 | 2,392 |
| 3 | 0.712 | | 9,000 | -4,000 | 5,000 | | 3,559 |
| 4 | 0.636 | | 9,000 | -4,000 | 5,000 | | 3,178 |
| 5 | 0.567 | | 8,000 | -4,000 | 4,000 | | 2,270 |
| | | | | | | **N P V =** | **3,291** |

## Expressing sensitivities

The question is how to determine and demonstrate in an intelligible manner the effect of changes in the parameters (estimates) one at a time. A good method of doing this is to express the maximum unfavourable change in a parameter as a percentage of the original estimate of the parameter, that is, the value of the parameter where the NPV becomes zero – in the example above a decrease of net present value of 3,291 can be tolerated. This present amount can then be related to the parameters one at a time.

By how much could the estimate of cost of the investment rise without the project being rejected?

For NPV to be zero, investment cost would have to rise by the amount of the NPV to 12,291 which is 36.56% more than the expected cost.

$$\frac{3{,}291}{9{,}000} = 36.56\%$$

The question can then be asked – is the estimate of original capital costs at all likely to be 36% out?

Sensitivity analysis is obviously more easily carried out with the use of spreadsheets.

| rate = | 12% | | | | | | |
|---|---|---|---|---|---|---|---|
| | | | cashflows: | | | | |
| | discount factor | cash out | cash in | cash out | net cash flow | | discounted cash flows |
| Year | | | | | | | |
| 0 | 1.000 | -12,291 | | | -12,291 | | -12,291 |
| 1 | 0.893 | | 2,000 | -1,000 | 1,000 | | 893 |
| 2 | 0.797 | | 6,000 | -3,000 | 3,000 | | 2,392 |
| 3 | 0.712 | | 9,000 | -4,000 | 5,000 | | 3,559 |
| 4 | 0.636 | | 9,000 | -4,000 | 5,000 | | 3,178 |
| 5 | 0.567 | | 8,000 | -4,000 | 4,000 | | 2,270 |
| | | 36.57% | 0.00% | 0.00% | | N P V = | 0 |

The example then goes on to show how the other parameters may be tested for sensitivity one at a time. A table of the results gives a useful overall guide to the sensitivity of the project. In the example the table of the three sensitive parameters has been compiled by trial and error and shows that with a fall in sales of 14.16% the NPV is zero. An important, obvious point is that the larger the parameter the more sensitive it will be. In this example cash in – the sales are almost twice the cash out, therefore any percentage change in cash in has almost twice the effect of an equal percentage change in cash out.

| rate = 12% | | | | | | | |
|---|---|---|---|---|---|---|---|
| | | | cashflows: | | | | |
| | discount | cash out | cash in | cash out | net | | discounted |
| | factor | | | | cash flow | | cash flows |
| Year | | | | | | | |
| 0 | 1.000 | -9,000 | | | -9,000 | | -9,000 |
| 1 | 0.893 | | 1,717 | -1,000 | 717 | | 640 |
| 2 | 0.797 | | 5,150 | -3,000 | 2,150 | | 1,714 |
| 3 | 0.712 | | 7,725 | -4,000 | 3,725 | | 2,652 |
| 4 | 0.636 | | 7,725 | -4,000 | 3,725 | | 2,368 |
| 5 | 0.567 | | 6,867 | -4,000 | 2,867 | | 1,627 |
| | | 0.00% | -14.16% | 0.00% | | N P V = | **0** |
| table of sensitivities | | 36.57% | -14.16% | 30.07% | | | |

This analysis is done not just to rule out sensitive projects, but should be considered in a more positive way, as a means of identifying potential problem areas and thus attempting to 'tie them down' and in some way minimise risk. An obvious limitation of the method is that not all parameters can be considered to change independently. In cases where parameters are inter-related then sensitivities can be considered over possible ranges of the related parameters.

## Method of capital budgeting and project appraisal

Many companies will have well established capital/project budgeting process, often linked to their annual operating budget process. Often the prime aim of the capital budget is to manage the scarce resource cash, that is to ration it in some way and hopefully select the best assets or projects in which to invest.

- **Identify likely assets or projects in which to invest** – linking the selection to the long-term objectives of the company.

- **Carry out screening appraisals**, particularly where there is a surfeit of likely investment opportunities.
- **Carry out detailed appraisals and sensitivity analysis.**
- **Review the projects.**

There should be a timetable for the performing of each stage and the stages should be subject to review. A good practice is to have presentations for funds made to a review panel.

Also, where regular appraisals have to be carried out it is good to have a manual or set of procedures, not bureaucracy, but rather guidance on the appraisal process. Examples of the stages of a typical company project which has successfully been appraised is useful guidance. The aim is to have thorough consistent appraisals.

## Capital expenditure budgeting – question

A company has two projects in which it might invest. It has sufficient funds for only one of the projects and thus both are to be appraised using the DCF measures, NPV and IRR.

If NPV is chosen as the principal measure which of the two investment options set out below should be chosen?

*What other matters should be considered?*

### *Project A*

Replace the existing factory compressor which supplies essential compressed air to the production process. The capital cost is 190,000 and there should be annual savings in electricity consumption of 38,000 and of maintenance of 19,000 per annum.

*Project B*

Replace the entire lighting systems in the factory and office accommodation at a cost of 177,000 with electricity consumption savings of 66,000 per annum, but additional bulb replacement and maintenance cost of 23,000 per annum from year 3 onward.

## Capital expenditure budgeting – feedback

| | | | | | | | | |
|---|---|---|---|---|---|---|---|---|
| | | required rate = | 15.00% | | | | | |
| **Project A** | | | | | | | | |
| | year | 0 | 1 | 2 | 3 | 4 | 5 | 6 |
| capital | | | | | | | | |
| | 190,000 | -190,000 | | | | | | |
| electricity savings | | | | | | | | |
| | 38,000 | | 38,000 | 38,000 | 38,000 | 38,000 | 38,000 | 38,000 |
| maintenance savings | | | | | | | | |
| | 19,000 | | 19,000 | 19,000 | 19,000 | 19,000 | 19,000 | 19,000 |
| net cash flow | | -190,000 | 57,000 | 57,000 | 57,000 | 57,000 | 57,000 | 57,000 |
| discount factor | | 1.0000 | 0.8696 | 0.7561 | 0.6575 | 0.5718 | 0.4972 | 0.4323 |
| discounted cash flow | | -190,000 | 49,565 | 43,100 | 37,478 | 32,590 | 28,339 | 24,643 |
| **NPV of project A =** | | **25,716** | | | | | | |
| | | | | | | | | |
| **Project B** | | | | | | | | |
| | year | 0 | 1 | 2 | 3 | 4 | 5 | 6 |
| capital | | | | | | | | |
| | 177,000 | -177,000 | | | | | | |
| electricity savings | | | | | | | | |
| | 66,000 | | 66,000 | 66,000 | 66,000 | 66,000 | 66,000 | 66,000 |
| maintenance costs | | | | | | | | |
| | 23,000 | | | | -23,000 | -23,000 | -23,000 | -23,000 |
| net cash flow | | -177,000 | 66,000 | 66,000 | 43,000 | 43,000 | 43,000 | 43,000 |
| discount factor | | 1.0000 | 0.8696 | 0.7561 | 0.6575 | 0.5718 | 0.4972 | 0.4323 |
| discounted cash flow | | -177,000 | 57,391 | 49,905 | 28,273 | 24,585 | 21,379 | 18,590 |
| **NPV of project B =** | | **23,124** | | | | | | |

When the IRRs are calculated Project A is 19.9% and project B 20.3%.

This reversal from a decision made on an NPV basis is due to the higher cash flows of Project B at the earlier stages - these cash flows are discounted the least and thus whilst there are subsequently lower cash flows giving a lower overall NPV it is the high early cash flows - payback which gives the higher NPV.

This example has been deliberately contrived to show this effect, generally a decision on which of one or more projects should be selected will be clear as both NPV and IRR will convey the same message.

For the above projects neither the NPVs or IRRs are spectacular nor different and before a decision was made the basic data would have to be checked carefully.

Certainly the costs savings and particularly the delayed staring of Bs replacement and maintenance costs should be checked.

### Summary

Models often do not give the answer, but do form a very valuable basis for decision making. They quantify the sensitivities of parameters and often indicate which data should be more thoroughly investigated before a final decision is reached.

## Checklist

- ✓ Cash is a scarce resource.
- ✓ There must be consistent method when appraising cash expenditure.
- ✓ A thorough sensitivity analysis should be carried out.

section one

# Costing for planning

What is costing?

Costing for planning

Checklist

## What is costing?

Costing can be a very confusing subject to study. Not because it or the individual definitions and accounting models are inherently complex, but rather the title implies one subject - costing, when in fact there are many definitions of the word 'cost' and many different models as businesses have to cost for different purposes.

Ask anyone what is meant by cost and the most common answer is 'the cost of a product or service', cost being what has to be paid for the material, components, labour and overheads necessarily incurred. This is what accountants call full cost, but is only one of several cost models met in business.

This text studies the three most relevant and common costing models. It is important at the outset to realise that although they may use common or similar definitions of cost and use the same basic data, the three models exist for quite disparate purposes. It is most important before discussing costing or getting involved in any costing exercise to be clear as to exactly what has to be costed and why.

**The three types of costing are as follows:**

### Full costing – coping with overheads

This is to most people the most obvious type of costing. It involves the building up of the cost of a unit or units of products or service. Many of the costs will be directly related to the product or service - **direct costs**, but others will have to be allocated, apportioned or absorbed to allow the total full cost to be determined. It is the allocation, apportionment or absorption of these **indirect costs**, more commonly called overheads, which may cause many real or often perceived problems.

## Costing for planning

When planning activities the costing exercise is more concerned with the long-term rather than the cost of one item at a particular point in time. It is really *macro* costing for overall planning and decision making. Planning is concerned with the longer term and whilst this may in some instances only be a month or less it is normally a year or longer period. Thus, for planning purposes, costs are considered as one of two types, **variable** - that is varying in proportion to different levels of activity and **fixed** - that is fixed over the period of time being studied.

## Costing for control

This costing is concerned with finding the cost of a unit or units of production or service and comparing these with actual costs incurred over a period. Any differences may indicate that the business is not performing as planned and corrective or remedial action is required (however it may be that the budgeted cost is wrong!). Costing for control can use direct costs only, utilise full costing - including all overheads or be carried out at some other level of detail.

Before proceeding to study any of the costing models it is important to understand the four basic definitions of costs and thus where they are relevant.

### 1 Direct cost

A cost which is indisputably related to the process, sales or output being considered. It is a cost which is not shared between two or more activities but is directly related to the product, project, process, service etc, being costed.

## 2 Indirect cost or overheads

A cost which cannot be easily, or at all, related to the product, project, process, service etc, being costed. It is a cost which often has to be shared between two or more activities - it has to be allocated to, apportioned to or absorbed into the product, project, process, service etc, being costed along with direct costs to give the full cost. Indirect costs are often called overheads.

## 3 Variable cost

A cost which varies with the product, project, process, service etc, being costed. It is a cost definition used in costing for planning, sometimes called marginal costing. As a starting point in planning exercises it is assumed that a variable cost will vary in direct proportion to changes in output - that is if 1 kg of material costs 3 then 4 kg will cost 12.

## 4 Fixed cost

A cost which is fixed in amount for a particular time period and over a range of activities. Overhead or indirect costs are often fixed in nature, for example the rent of a factory will be fixed for, say, one year at least, no matter how many products are made in the factory. The rent could change next year and a larger factory would presumably increase the rental charge. *Fixed costs can be variable!*

As a start point in planning exercises it is assumed that indirect costs are absolutely fixed (over a range or activity and a specified time period).

# Costing for planning

A cash flow forecast demonstrates that there are often direct (cash) costs in business. The use of one range of non varying direct (cash) costs is appropriate for a basic cash flow forecast, but in planning a businesses activities consideration must be given to the different possible levels of sales, output or production and the fact that in real life there are costs which are fixed.

Costing for planning, also called marginal costing deals with the fact that some costs are fixed (at least over a range of output and over a period of time) and some vary. Marginal costing models are concerned with investigating the behaviour of fixed and variable costs over ranges.

Firstly definitions of variable and fixed cost should be reviewed.

### *Variable cost*

A cost which varies with the product, project, process, service etc, being costed. It is a cost definition used in costing for planning, sometimes called marginal costing. As a starting point in planning exercises it is assumed that a variable cost will vary in direct proportion to changes in output – that is if 1 kg of material costs 3 then 4 kg will cost 12.

### *Fixed cost*

A cost which is fixed in amount for a particular time period and over a range of activities. Overhead or indirect costs are often fixed in nature, for example the rent of a factory will be fixed for, say, one year at least, no matter how many products are made in the factory. The rent could change next year and a larger factory would presumably increase the rental charge. *Fixed costs can be variable!*

As a start point in planning exercises it is assumed that indirect costs are absolutely fixed (over a range or activity and a specified time period).

## Basic planning model – marginal costing and break-even model

### Illustration

A company makes one product which it sells for 9. The costs of production are as follows:

| | | |
|---|---|---|
| Labour assembly cost per product | 2.5 | |
| Components per product | 4.5 | |
| Total variable costs | 7.0 | |
| Total fixed costs of assembly area for one year | | 4,000 |
| Selling or transfer price | 9.0 | |
| Variable costs | -7.0 | |
| Contribution or contribution margin | 2.0 | |
| Total fixed costs | 4,000.0 | |
| divide by contribution | 2.0 | |

Gives 2,000 items have to be made and sold to cover the overheads or 2,000 items have to be made and sold to **break-even**.

It is most important to realise that simple as this may seem, this is really all there is to the marginal costing and break-even model – it is only the volume of data and sophistication which makes the subject seem complex at times. Section 2 covers marginal costing in more detail.

## Break-even – question

A couple are contemplating opening a small restaurant serving snacks and light meals.

They have collected the following data on costs and research suggests that the average sales per customer will be 4.

Operating costs – annual figures

| | |
|---|---:|
| Wages | 31,500 |
| Rent | 6,000 |
| Rates | 2,200 |
| Insurance | 500 |
| Heat/light | 2,000 |
| Phone | 500 |
| Stationery | 200 |
| Sundry | 400 |

Cost of sales will be 30% of sales value, that is there is a 70% margin on sales.

They require to know how many customers are needed in an average five day week if they are to break-even. It is assumed there will be 50 working weeks in the year.

There is the option of opening for seven days a week. Only wages and heat and light would increase pro rata, that is to 7/5ths of the present figure.

What is the required average number of customers to break-even with seven day opening?

## Restaurant break-even – feedback

| | Five day week annual figures | Seven day week annual figures |
|---|---|---|
| Wages | 31,500 | 44,100 |
| Rent | 6,000 | 6,000 |
| Rates | 2,200 | 2,200 |
| Insurance | 500 | 500 |
| Heat/light | 2,000 | 2,800 |
| Phone | 500 | 500 |
| Stationery | 300 | 300 |
| Sundry | 400 | 400 |
| total fixed costs | 43,400 | 56,800 |
| gross profit required to cover fixed costs | 43,400 | 56,800 |
| sales value required (required gross profit/0.7) | 62,000 | 81,143 |
| annual number of customers at 4 each | **15,500** | **20,286** |
| average daily number of customers | 62 | 58 |

This exercise would let the potential restaurateurs research whether it was likely that such an establishment would hit the level of daily or weekly customers.

It can be seen that as many costs are fixed the average number of customers per day is less with seven day working. However, research would have to be carried out to see if the two quietest days would generate sufficient business.

## Checklist

- ✓ Know your cost behaviour and definitions.
- ✓ Marginal costing is a planning model.
- ✓ Costs are considered as fixed or variable.
- ✓ Break-even occurs where fixed costs are covered.

# Costing for planning

## Detailed planning and break-even analysis

## Checklist

## Detailed planning and break-even analysis

To carry out a detailed break-even analysis for planning purposes break-even charts may be produced and sensitivity analysis carried out. Spreadsheets are obvious means of carrying out the sensitivity analysis.

Using the figures from the simple example in Section 1, break-even analysis can be carried out in a more detailed way.

| | | |
|---|---|---|
| product selling price | 9.0 | |
| labour assembly cost per product | 2.5 | |
| components per product | 4.5 | |
| total variable costs | 7.0 | |
| total fixed costs of assembly area for one year | | 4,000 |
| selling or transfer price | 9.0 | |
| variable costs | -7.0 | |
| contribution or contribution margin | **2.0** | |
| total fixed costs | 4,000.0 | |
| divide by contribution | 2.0 | |

gives 2,000 items have to be made and sold to cover the overheads or 2,000 items have to be made and sold to **break-even**.

Set out on the following pages is a spreadsheet solution of the above illustration. This goes on to show how the parameters may be varied to understand more of the situation being assessed.

**Marginal costing - break even analysis**

| | | | | | |
|---|---|---|---|---|---|
| Selling price | SP | **9.00** | Contribution | M=SP-VC | **2.00** |
| Variable costs | | | Break even | FC/M | **2000** |
| labour | | 2.50 | no of units | | |
| materials | | 4.50 | | | |
| | VC | **7.00** | | | |
| Fixed costs | FC | **4000** | | | |

revenue and costs for a range of units

| no of units | 0 | 500 | 1000 | 1500 | 2000 | 2500 | 3000 | 3500 |
|---|---|---|---|---|---|---|---|---|
| fixed costs | 4000 | 4000 | 4000 | 4000 | 4000 | 4000 | 4000 | 4000 |
| variable costs | 0 | 3500 | 7000 | 10500 | 14000 | 17500 | 21000 | 24500 |
| total costs | 4000 | 7500 | 11000 | 14500 | 18000 | 21500 | 25000 | 28500 |
| selling price | 0 | 4500 | 9000 | 13500 | 18000 | 22500 | 27000 | 31500 |

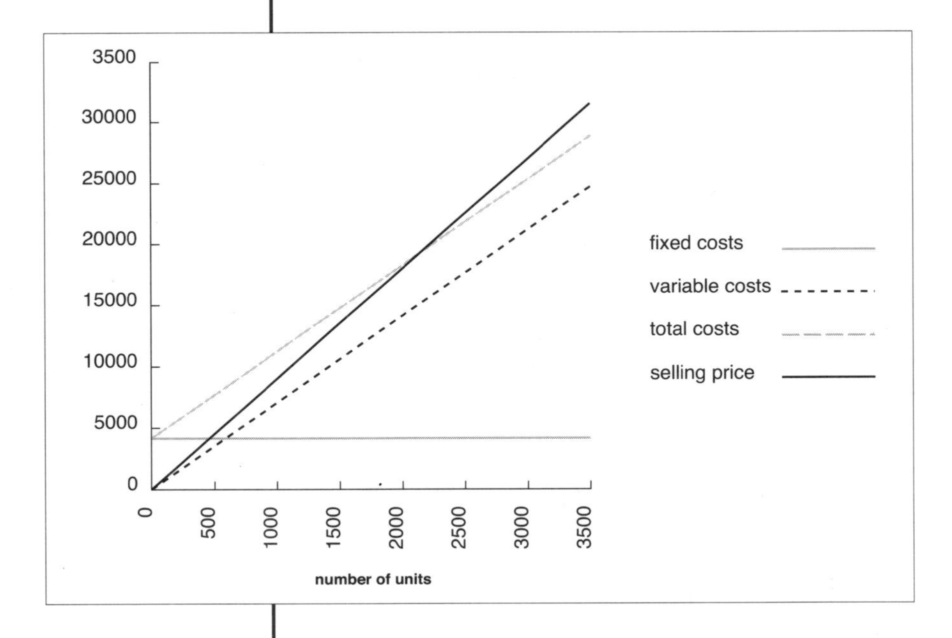


The example on this page shows the key parameters, revenue/income, sales, variable costs, contribution or margin being revenue less variable costs, and fixed costs. The example goes on to show how revenue and cost behaviour can be calculated over a range of sales or output. This gives rise to three 'curves' on the chart. A revenue line starting from 0, a fixed cost line – a straight line at the level of the fixed costs, a total cost line – being the slope of variable costs but starting from the fixed cost level. The point at which revenue and total costs intersect gives the break-even revenue figure and also the number of break-even units.

It may be clearer to show only two curves, one being the slope of the contribution or margin and the other the fixed cost line. The point at which these two lines intersect again gives the break-even number of units (but it does not give the break-even revenue).

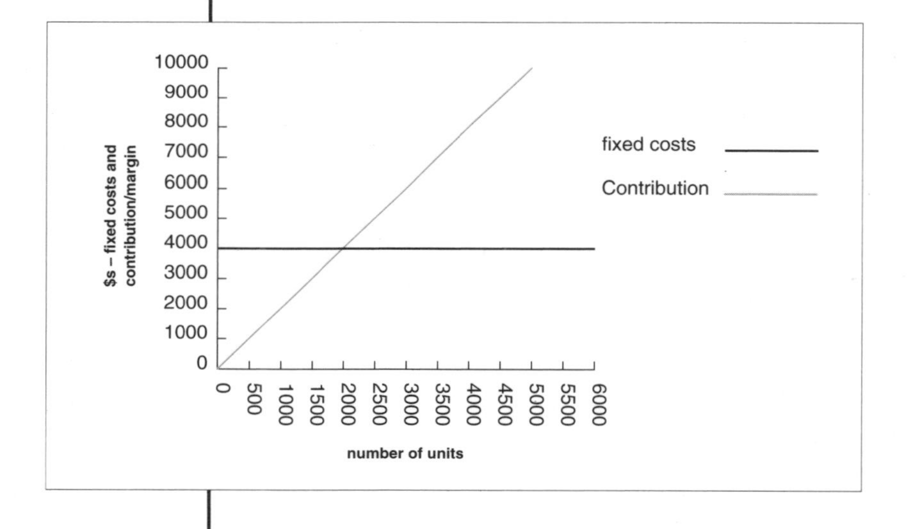


The basic model may then be used to analyse many possible permutations of parameters. For example:

a) What happens if fixed costs increase by 10%?

b) With fixed costs of 4,000 how many units have to be sold to give a profit of 1,000?

c) If fixed costs increase by 10% and revenue per unit falls by 15%, how many items have to be made and sold to break-even?

## Marginal costing – break-even analysis

### *Sensitivity analysis – basic model*

| | | | sensitivity change | | | | |
|---|---|---|---|---|---|---|---|
| Selling price | SP | 9.00 | 0% | 9.00 | Contribution | M = SP-VC | 2.00 |
| Variable costs | | | | | Break-even | = FC/M | 2000 |
| labour | | 2.50 | 0% | 2.50 | no of units | | |
| materials | | 4.50 | 0% | 4.50 | No of units | = P/M | 0 |
| | VC | 7.00 | | 7.00 | to yield profit | | |
| Fixed costs | FC | 4000 | 0% | 4000 | | | |
| Profit | P | 0 | 0% | 0 | (FC+P)/M | 2000 | |

**a)**

| | | | | | | | |
|---|---|---|---|---|---|---|---|
| Selling price | SP | 9.00 | 0% | 9.00 | Contribution | M = SP-VC | 2.00 |
| Variable costs | | | | | Break-even | = FC/M | 2200 |
| labour | | 2.50 | 0% | 2.50 | no of units | | |
| materials | | 4.50 | 0% | 4.50 | No of units | = P/M | 0 |
| | VC | 7.00 | | 7.00 | to yield profit | | |
| Fixed costs | FC | 4000 | 10% | 4400 | | | |
| Profit | P | 0 | 0% | 0 | (FC+P)/M | | 2200 |

**b)**

| | | | | | | | |
|---|---|---|---|---|---|---|---|
| Selling price | SP | 9.00 | 0% | 9.00 | Contribution | M = SP-VC | 2.00 |
| Variable costs | | | | | Break-even | = FC/M | 2000 |
| labour | | 2.50 | 0% | 2.50 | no of units | | |
| materials | | 4.50 | 0% | 4.50 | No of units | = P/M | 500 |
| | VC | 7.00 | | 7.00 | to yield profit | | |
| Fixed costs | FC | 4000 | 0% | 4000 | | | |
| Profit | P | 1000 | 0% | 1000 | (FC+P)/M | | 2500 |

**c)**

| | | | | | | | |
|---|---|---|---|---|---|---|---|
| Selling price | SP | 9.00 | -15% | 7.65 | Contribution | M = SP-VC | 0.65 |
| Variable costs | | | | | Break-even | = FC/M | 6769 |
| labour | | 2.50 | 0% | 2.50 | no of units | | |
| materials | | 4.50 | 0% | 4.50 | No of units | = P/M | 1538 |
| | VC | 7.00 | | 7.00 | to yield profit | | |
| Fixed costs | FC | 4000 | 10% | 4400 | | | |
| Profit | P | 1000 | 0% | 1000 | (FC+P)/M | | 8308 |

In the above example the basic data is entered in the left hand column and the right hand column is then simply the basic input data multiplied by 1+% sensitivity change entered in the middle column. Therefore for a) fixed costs go up by 10% from the base 4,000 to 4,400 and this has the effect of increasing the break-even number to 2,200 units.

If this model is laid out on a spreadsheet then obviously endless sensitivity analysis can be quickly carried out.

If we take the example of an established business which has good knowledge of its manufacturing process, costing and revenues, and wished to see how it may expand by producing an extension to the present range of products, it is not only the cash requirements for this which are important (the business will still have to produce an up to date cash flow forecast) but, more fundamentally, a review of whether the expansion should be undertaken at all – the business will have to budget/plan to see if the proposal is viable as a business with the expected levels of activity (production and sales) and costs.

An example of the data required for planning purposes is set out below:

## Break-even analysis

| *Fixed costs* | | | *Variable costs* | | |
|---|---|---|---|---|---|
| | | sensitivity | | | sensitivity |
| a | 1000 | 0.00% | c | 40 | 0.00% |
| b | 3000 | 0.00% | d | 160 | 0.00% |
| total | 4000 | | total | 200 | |
| Revenue | | Volumes | | x units | |
| | 300 | 0.00% | | | |

| per unit | |
|---|---|
| Revenue | 300 |
| Variable costs | 200 |
| Contribution Margin | 100 |
| Fixed costs | 4000 |
| break-even | 40 units |

This model has all the basic information required to carry out a break-even analysis. The basic data is for the production of one unit but likely volumes of production can be entered in the 'Volumes' column.There will, of course, be much more detail of cost/revenue build up in a real life example.

The model is set up with a simple method of carrying out a sensitivity analysis of the input parameters – the effect of using these is shown below:

### Break-even analysis – sensitivity analysis

| *Fixed costs* | | | *Variable costs* | | |
|---|---|---|---|---|---|
| | | sensitivity | | | sensitivity |
| a | 1000 | 100.00% | c | 40 | 0.00% |
| b | 3000 | 0.00% | d | 160 | 0.00% |
| total | 4000 | | total | 200 | |
| Revenue | | Volumes | | x units | |
| | 300 | 0.00% | | | |

| per unit | | |
|---|---|---|
| Revenue | 300 | |
| Variable costs | 200 | |
| Contribution margin | 100 | |
| Fixed costs | 5000 | |
| break-even | 50 | units |

In the example above only one of the fixed costs has been increased – by 100%. The effect on the model is obvious. This process could be repeated and a table or charts of the effect of changes in the various parameters prepared.

## Break-even analysis – question

A company is proposing to make a new picnic product whose sales will of course be highly dependent on the weather. The marketing department is also not sure as to whether to make this a high margin item, in which case lower sales could be tolerated, or to go for low margin (lower price) and thus require higher volume of sales.

Data for the fixed and variable costs of manufacturing the product are set out below:

a) With the base data, how many items need to be sold to break-even?

b) What selling price would be required if only 5,000 items were sold and a profit of at least 10,000 was required from the new product?

c) How many items would have to be sold if the selling price was set at 9.99

| | | |
|---|---|---|
| base selling price | 12.00 | per unit |
| assembly | 3.50 | per unit |
| components | 2.80 | per unit |
| inspection | 0.70 | per unit |
| fabric | 2.50 | per unit |
| fixed assembly area costs | 12000 | |
| equipment depreciation | 4000 | |
| materials handling costs | 2000 | |

## Break-even analysis – feedback

a) With the base data, how many items need to be sold to break-even?

| | | | | | |
|---|---|---|---|---|---|
| Selling price | | | 12.00 | Fixed costs | |
| | | | | | 12,000 |
| Variable costs | | | | | 4,000 |
| | assembly | 3.50 | | | 2,000 |
| | components | 2.80 | | **total** | **18,000** |
| | inspection | 0.70 | | | |
| | fabric | 2.50 | | number of units to break-even | |
| | | | 9.50 | | |
| | contribution margin | | **2.50** | = | 7,200 |

b) What selling price would be required if only 5,000 items were sold and a profit of at least 10,000 was required from the new product?

| | | | | | |
|---|---|---|---|---|---|
| Selling price | | | **15.10** | Fixed costs | |
| | | | | | 12,000 |
| Variable costs | | | | | 4,000 |
| | assembly | 3.50 | | | 2,000 |
| | components | 2.80 | | **total** | **18,000** |
| | inspection | 0.70 | | profit | 10,000 |
| | fabric | 2.50 | | | 28,000 |
| | | | 9.50 | | |
| | | contribution margin | **5.60** | contribution per unit to give 1,000 profit | |

$$= \frac{28,000}{5,000} = 5.60$$

c) How many items would have to be sold if the selling price was set at 9.99?

| | | | | | |
|---|---|---|---|---|---|
| Selling price | | | 9.99 | Fixed costs | |
| | | | | | 12,000 |
| Variable costs | | | | | 4,000 |
| | assembly | 3.50 | | | 2,000 |
| | components | 2.80 | | **total** | **18,000** |
| | inspection | 0.70 | | | |
| | fabric | 2.50 | | number of units to break-even | |
| | | | 9.50 | | |
| | contribution margin | | **0.49** | = | 36,735 |

The results of this limited sensitivity analysis reveal that to sell at a low price 9.99 means a great increase in volumes from the base position. The prime question must be 'is this possible?'

The above analysis can be developed with much more detail and with sensitivities of all relevant and material parameters reviewed for sensitivity.

Much is made in management account text books of the need to be aware of limited resources and thus to work out which mix of products which consume limited resources will yield maximum overall margin.

There are little 'sums' that can be done to indicate the mix of products which yields the maximum margin, but what these traditional exercises often missed was the point that it is not the limited resource which is the problem so much as what the market demands.

With the use of spreadsheets it is possible to review a wide range of possible scenarios which will use scarce resources to best effect, whilst also meeting as far as possible market demands.

## Summary

### *An approach to break-even analysis*

- Set down (with the aid of your team) all income and cost headings
- Ensure all costs are relevant
- Check for omissions
- Identify cost behaviour - fixed or variable (or a mix)
- Draft the model layout
- Think (get the team to think) of what are sensitive parameters and what likely outcomes might be - **don't rely on the spreadsheet – use business sense – the spreadsheet is there as an aid**
- Set up a model which can be used for sensitivity analysis
- Carry out a thorough sensitivity analysis

- Review the outcomes
- Can the model be improved – is more detailed analysis required?

## Checklist

- ✓ Know your cost behaviour and definitions.
- ✓ Consider short and long-term costs.
- ✓ Are all costs relevant?
- ✓ Marginal costing is a planning tool.

# Costing

What is costing?

Full costing – coping with overheads

Problems of overhead allocation

Dealing with the problems

Checklist

## What is costing?

Costing can be a very confusing subject to study. Not because it or the individual definitions and accounting models are inherently complex, but rather the title implies one subject – costing – when in fact there are many definitions of the word 'cost' and many different models as businesses have to cost for different purposes.

Ask anyone what is meant by cost and the most common answer is 'the cost of a product or service,' cost being what has to be paid for the material, components, labour and overheads necessarily incurred. This is what accountants call **full** cost, but is only one of several cost models met in business.

This text studies the three most relevant and common costing models. It is important at the outset to realise that although they may use common or similar definitions of cost and use the same basic data, the three models exist for quite disparate purposes. It is most important before discussing costing or getting involved in any costing exercise to be clear as to exactly what has to be costed and why.

***The three types of costing are as follows:***

### Full costing – coping with overheads

This is to most people the most obvious type of costing. It involves the building up of the cost of a unit or units of products or service. Many of the costs will be directly related to the product or service – **direct costs**, but others will have to be allocated, apportioned or absorbed to allow the total full cost to be determined. It is the allocation, apportionment or absorption of these **indirect costs**, more commonly called overheads, which may cause many real or often perceived problems.

## Costing for planning

When planning activities, the costing exercise is more concerned with the long-term rather than the cost of one item at a particular point in time. It is really macro costing for overall planning and decision making. Planning is concerned with the longer term and whilst this may in some instances be only a month or less, it is normally a year or longer period. Thus, for planning purposes, costs are considered as one of two types, **variable** - that is varying in proportion to different levels of activity and **fixed** - that is fixed over the period of time being studied.

## Costing for control

This costing is concerned with finding the cost of a unit or units of production or service and comparing these with actual costs incurred over a period. Any differences may indicate that the business is not performing as planned and corrective or remedial action is required (however it may be that the budgeted cost is wrong!). Costing for control can use direct costs only, utilise full costing - including all overheads or be carried out at some other level of detail.

Before proceeding to study any of the costing models it is important to understand the four basic costs' definitions and thus where they are relevant.

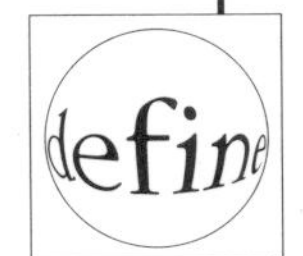


### 1 Direct cost

A cost which is indisputably related to the process, sales or output being considered. It is a cost which is not shared between two or more activities but is directly related to the product, project, process, service etc, being costed.

## 2 Indirect cost or overheads

A cost which cannot be easily, or at all, related to the product, project, process, service etc, being costed. It is a cost which often has to be shared between two or more activities – it has to be allocated to, apportioned to or absorbed into the product, project, process, service etc, being costed along with direct costs to give the full cost. Indirect costs are often called overheads.

## 3 Variable cost

A cost which varies with the product, project, process, service etc, being costed. It is a cost definition used in costing for planning, sometimes called marginal costing. As a starting point in planning exercises it is assumed that a variable cost will vary in direct proportion to changes in output – that is if 1kg of material costs $3 then 4kg will cost $12.

## 4 Fixed cost

A cost which is fixed in amount for a particular time period and over a range of activities. Overhead or indirect costs are often fixed in nature, for example the rent of a factory will be fixed for, say, one year at least, no matter how many products are made in the factory. The rent could change next year and a larger factory would presumably increase the rental charge. *Fixed costs can be variable!*

As a start point in planning exercises it is assumed that indirect costs are absolutely fixed (over a range or activity and a specified time period).

# Full costing – coping with overheads

Full or absorption costing is concerned with calculating the 'correct' total or full cost for a product, process or service.

## Definitions appropriate to full or absorption costing

### *Direct cost*

A cost which is indisputably related to the process, sales or output being considered. It is a cost which is not shared between two or more activities but is directly related to the product, project, process, service etc, being costed.

### *Indirect cost or overheads*

A cost which cannot be easily, or at all, related to the product, project, process, service etc, being costed. It is a cost which often has to be shared between two or more activities – it has to be allocated to, apportioned to or absorbed into the product, project, process, service etc, being costed along with direct costs to give the full cost. Indirect costs are often called overheads.

Ideally, all costs would be direct costs, in which case there would be few or no arguments over what something cost. The concept of running projects, departments etc as profit or at least cost centres with cross charging of costs aims to turn what may be indirect costs (overheads) into direct costs.

This is also the principle behind internal markets in goods and services, which may lead to comparisons with outside suppliers who, if cheaper, may lead a company to out source.

However, any business will have costs which necessarily have to be incurred and which are indirect to a specific product or service. These are indirect costs, more commonly called overheads or burden. They have to be taken into account and charged to products or services or recovered from products or services. Indirect or overhead costs form part of the cost of a product or service.

There are many different types of business where the full cost has to be determined for pricing, decision making and control purposes. Examples where full costing, with the inclusion of overheads, are as follows:

### *Job/project costing*

Each job/contract is unique. Therefore, direct costs plus relevant overheads are charged to an individual job, eg:

- building construction
- ship-building

### *Batch costing*

All items in a batch are identical. Therefore, direct costs plus relevant overheads are charged to a batch. The cost of each individual item is the cost of the batch divided by the number of items produced, eg:

- small electric motors
- bakery products

### *Process costing*

Items produced are very similar and involve identical processes. Direct costs plus relevant overheads are charged to the process. The cost of each item is the total cost of each process for a period divided by the number of units produced during the period, eg:

- manufacture of chemical cleaners

All of the above will have some element of their costs being indirect to the activity and thus these have to be charged to, allocated to, apportioned to, or recovered from the product or service. Note that there are many possible words which might be used. Also the word *relevant* has been used to make the point that what overheads are allocated depends on what managers consider to be relevant.

The major elements of direct costs of production are direct materials and direct labour. The methods require a system involving time sheets, job cards, stock requisition notes, etc. The only major difference between manufacturing and service industries is that the former involve high material costs whereas the latter involve mainly wage/salary costs.

g

## Job or project costing

Each job is considered on its own.

Direct labour materials and overheads are costed and indirect overheads are allocated on some pre-determined basis.

| | Job 7157 |
|---|---|
| **Materials** | |
| Steel and fastenings | 27,160 |
| **Labour** | |
| Machining | 4,100 |
| Assembly | 10,260 |
| **Direct overheads** | 4,010 |
| **Total direct costs** | **45,530** |

To these the overhead costs have to be added on some predetermined basis.

| | |
|---|---|
| Indirect overheads | |
| 150% Labour cost machining | 6,150 |
| Total job cost | **51,680** |

This method is meant to give the 'true' cost of a job. If quantities are correctly determined, costing is accurate and overheads properly allocated or absorbed, the cost may be very nearly correct and can be used as a basis for pricing jobs and subsequent short-term control.

A major problem is obviously the subjective area of overhead allocation/absorption/apportionment.

### Indirect costs (overheads)

Having decided the method to be used for accumulating direct production costs, the difficulty which arises with all costing methods is indirect costs (overheads) allocation.

Overheads to be allocated to production can be split as follows:

- Indirect costs of production eg factory heat and light, factory cleaning; and
- Costs of service departments eg cost of factory restaurant, cost of wages department.

There is no way that these costs can be directly costed to a job, contract, batch or process and, therefore, some fair basis of spreading the overheads must be chosen.

### Overhead allocation/absorption

This is a topic with which both the accountant and the manager may get bogged down!

What is overhead allocation?

### Overhead allocation

What is overhead allocation, apportionment, absorption or any other appropriate term for sharing out the overheads (often fixed costs) of a business?

The following example illustrates just three of the possibly infinite number of ways by which overheads might be shared.

**Three products, projects or types of service**

| cost components | K | L | M | total costs |
|---|---|---|---|---|
| Labour | 20 | 40 | 60 | 120 |
| Materials | 50 | 10 | 20 | 80 |
| Sub contract | 10 | 30 | 0 | 40 |
| Total costs | 80 | 80 | 80 | 240 |
| | | | overheads = | 120 |
| | | | total full cost of the three products = | 360 |

**Overheads of 120 allocated on the basis of labour content**
labour as a fraction of total labour cost

| | K | L | M | total |
|---|---|---|---|---|
| | 1/6 | 1/3 | 1/2 | |
| overhead allocated | 20 | 40 | 60 | 120 |

**Overheads of 120 allocated on the basis of materials content**
materials as a fraction of total materials cost

| | K | L | M | total |
|---|---|---|---|---|
| overhead allocated | 5/8 | 1/8 | 1/4 | |
| | 75 | 15 | 30 | 120 |

**Overheads of 120 allocated on the basis of sub-contract content**
sub-contract as a fraction of total sub-contract cost

| | K | L | M | total |
|---|---|---|---|---|
| overhead allocated | 1/4 | 3/4 | 0 | |
| | 30 | 90 | 0 | 120 |

The full cost of the three products, projects or service will be 360 no matter which basis of allocation is used. K,L and M will have quite different costs

| costs of 80 plus overheads allocated on the basis of: | K | L | M | **total full costs** |
|---|---|---|---|---|
| **Labour** | 100 | 120 | 140 | **360** |
| **Materials** | 155 | 95 | 110 | **360** |
| **Sub contract** | 110 | 170 | 80 | **360** |

The above example illustrates that in essence overhead allocation is a simple exercise of collecting the overhead costs (often fixed), dividing them by an appropriate base figure to yield an overhead cost per unit of product or service. But in practice questions arise:

- What costs should be included as overheads?
- What base figure should be used?
- What is the size of the base?
- What happens if the volume of business changes?
- What base(s) should be used if there are many products or services?

The list of practical difficulties, real or perceived, may be many. However overheads are a fact of business life and have to be dealt with – as simply as possible. It may be a difficult area but it is worth noting that most successful companies take a pragmatic approach, keeping the overhead allocation exercise as simple as possible and not attempting to finesse their overhead allocation.

## Problems of overhead allocation

The problems of overhead allocation or absorption may be considered under three headings:

**Choosing a fair basis for allocation**

**The amount of overheads**

**Estimating volume of business**

### Choosing a fair basis for allocation

The apparent unfairness of overhead allocation is probably the most common 'whinge' from managers. They are quite correct to be concerned about overheads which are unfairly allocated where the unfairness is patently wrong.

The above example of overhead allocation demonstrates that if the wrong basis is chosen then quite wrong costs are calculated and thus wrong business decisions will be made.

## The amount of overheads

Firstly, there is the question of what should be included as overheads.The simple conventional answer which links with the financial accounting concept of prudence is that it is only normal factory or office overheads which are included. But what is normal? The idea is that it will be overheads which are necessarily incurred in producing products or providing a service.Thus general office overheads would be excluded from the overhead allocation to factory products. Further examples are marketing and research and development costs as these do not add value directly to the product or service being sold. Of course they should and usually do add value, but it is the concept that the costs are covered only when products or services are finally sold which means that these costs are left out of any overhead cost collection.

The second point is what is the correct amount or level of overheads? The answer must be none! Whilst impractical, this is the correct answer in theory. This is the argument behind profit centres, internal markets and out sourcing - turn nebulous, ever increasing overheads into direct costs and all will be well! You get better accountability.

## Estimating volume of business

This is the most difficult of the three problems as for many businesses overheads have to allocated in advance, based on assumptions of output.

However, many managers make too much of the problem - they know what the output for the next accounting period(s) will be, for example a construction company ought to have contracts in place for the next year (s) and thus should have an expected level of activity - volume of man hours.

## Dealing with the problems

g

### Choosing a fair basis for allocation

The fundamental premise should be to keep the basis of allocation as simple as possible.

This may mean using the traditional methods of using labour hours worked as a base where labour is the principal user of the overhead facilities or machine hours where machine use is the principal cause of overhead costs. An illustration of choosing appropriate basis can be found at the end of this chapter.

It may be that overheads are of quite distinct types and the business processes dictate that overheads be allocated on more than one basis. There is simply more work involved in cost analysis and subsequent number crunching. The ultimate development of this approach is to carry out an activity based costing (ABC) exercise - see Section 2.

Another detailed approach, possible for many situations, is to record or log all overhead costs and relate them in money terms to products, projects or service. For example, have all phone calls logged to projects, all photo copying charged to projects, overhead function time recorded down to say five minute intervals and charged to projects. The aim of this approach is to turn indirect overheads into direct costs and thus bring more accuracy and accountability. There is the need to have a reliable system, which cannot be abused in any way.

The other ultimate extreme from seeking detailed accuracy is not to allocate overheads at all. That is to cost projects, products and services with direct costs only and as long as an adequate contribution or margin is achieved for a sufficient volume of business overheads will be covered. This approach has the merit of simplicity, but really does not meet the criteria of giving the cost of a project product or service unit. The level to which overheads are analysed and costed into products is discussed in more detail in Section 2.

A simple approach of overhead allocation which would work for some businesses, such as contracting, would be to collect the overheads, and at say a weekly meeting have a representative group simply allocate on a fair basis. The group would have to be managed and have no prejudices. Another benefit of this approach is that it permits the, say weekly, review of the level of overheads prior to allocation. The amount of overheads being incurred is kept under constant review.

### The amount of overheads

The overheads should be reviewed critically - at the time they are being budgeted and a zero based approach as outlined in Chapter 10 Section 2 may help in this respect.

Often when the overheads are seen as being too high in amount it is the amount which has been allocated to a project, product or service which is too high. This problem has to be addressed, but if the recipient of the high level of overhead cannot challenge the amount then the business must have some process and staff responsible for critically reviewing the amount of overheads. Again an ABC approach may help in this respect.

### Estimating volume of business

This is the most difficult problem to manage. When accounting for overheads the volume of business - the predicted level of activity - will always depend on someone's forecast, marketing, production etc. The accuracy of the overhead per unit will only be as accurate as the forecast on which the arithmetic is based.

## Overheads – question

The budget figures for Z Ltd's factory for the year to 30 June 2xx7 are as follows:

| **Production** | |
|---|---|
| Machine hours* | 28,000 |
| Labour hours | 20,500 |
| Units of production | 14,000 |

| **Costs** | |
|---|---|
| Depreciation | 6,000 |
| Rates/local taxes | 3,200 |
| Electricity | 16,800 |
| Consumables | 8,800 |
| Supervision | 55,000 |
| (*3,000 labour hours included above) | |
| Share of security costs | 4,000 |
| Share of administration costs | 7,000 |
| **TOTAL COSTS** | 100,800 |

**Required**

1 Calculate an overhead allocation rate for the year using machine hours, direct labour hours and units of production.

2 What are the disadvantages of using a units of production overhead allocation basis?

3 Using the units of production basis, consider the following:

- No stock at 1 July 2xx6
- 1,000 completed units of stock at 30 June 2xx7
- Production in the year only 12,000 units (including the 1,000 stock units)
- What might you infer about machining costs and closing stock valuation for the year to 30 June 2xx7?

## Overheads – feedback

1a) Machine hours $\frac{\text{Relevant overheads}}{\text{Machine hours}}$ $\frac{93{,}800^{*}}{28{,}000}$

= £3.35/machine hour

General overheads have been omitted as these are not costs incurred in the production process – they are not part of the cost of the items produced. General overheads have to be written off as incurred – this is the prudence concept in action. This does of course mean that there has to be sufficient, gross factory or production profit to cover the general overheads which are not allocated to or absorbed into production.

b) Labour hours $\frac{93{,}800}{17{,}500}$

= £5.36/labour hour

c) Units of production $\frac{93{,}800}{14{,}000}$

= £6.7/unit

2) The major disadvantage is that the units of production method assumes absolute uniformity of production units.

3) Machining costs per unit are understated by

$\frac{93{,}800}{12{,}000}$ = 7.82 – 6.7 = £1.12 per unit

The practical effect of the lower production is that 2,000 units worth of overheads have not been recovered. They are 'under-recovered' or 'under-absorbed' and this will have to be written off as a loss in the P & L account.

Stock would also be understated in cost and hence value, but as production is down on that budgeted there must be questions over the realisable value of production.

## Checklist

- ✓ Challenge amounts of overheads.
- ✓ Use a simple fair basis of allocation.

# Costing

## How detailed should costing be?

## Activity based costing

## Checklist

## How detailed should costing be?

Before considering a contemporary approach to improve full costing and as an introduction before considering the latest method of costing, it is important to accept that there will probably be little fundamentally new in any costing techniques. This is the case as there are only direct costs or indirect costs - overheads.

The methods of costing are thus:

### 1 Only cost with direct costs

Control overheads as a separate exercise and do not attempt to allocate them. Forecast, hope that there will be sufficient contribution or margin to cover the overheads and deliver the desired net profit.

There can be no arguments over the accuracy of this method, but there may be questions over the management of the overheads and the forecasts of volume of business.

### 2 Fully cost with direct cost

Turn all costs into direct costs or have a highly accurate, painstakingly allocated overhead allocation system - the ultimate in activity based costing - see below.

Again there should be no arguments with this method.

### 3 An intermediate level of costing accuracy

Obviously cost in the direct costs and some amount of overhead. There are many possibilities here. The idea is to have as much detail and therefore as accurate costing as possible, but at the same time keep the exercise simple to give clarity and accountability to the process.

# Activity based costing

## Introduction

*Activity based costing – ABC*
*What is the issue?*

One way of identifying what ABC is about is to consider all the words which may be used in relation to the methods of including an element of overhead in a product or service unit – how 'full' costing is achieved.

Overhead costs or burden may be allocated, absorbed, apportioned, applied, etc, to a product or service unit and along with the direct costs they give the full cost.

The word 'allocation' might be used by the accountant who has an amount of overheads to distribute – he might (hopefully with some thought and discussion) find a basis for allocating them or 'handing them out'. The point is that the word allocate does imply a degree of arbitrariness about how the process is carried out – costs are just allocated – the accountant's ledgers are balanced and all is well!

The word 'absorbed' might be used where product (direct) costs are analysed. Products are reviewed to see what overhead facilities they cause and use and then the overheads are absorbed into the products to give the full cost.

Both words end with the desired result – overheads being spread, allocated to units of product or service. The more diligent exercise of absorbing overheads as described above is closer to what ABC aims to achieve. In spite of the new terms introduced, ABC is really just thoughtful, detailed overhead absorption (or you could say allocation). A problem that will become evident is that it is prone to the common management accountant's weakness of attempting to be too detailed with a view to obtaining unnecessary, or unobtainable, accuracy.

A declared major difference between ABC and conventional costing is in ABC treatment of non-volume related overhead costs and it is thus where non-volume related overheads are significant that the greatest benefit of the ABC approach may arise.

ABC was originally seen as being of most relevance for manufacturing situations and the earliest published studies relate to manufacturing. However, it is possible for the ABC approach to be used for overheads other than those of production, examples being selling, distribution and servicing departments - the principal driver for these may often be customer demand levels.

## Differences between ABC and conventional costing

For both conventional and ABC, costs are bundled together or pooled and then one or more overhead cost recovery rates used to allocate the pool of costs to the products.

So what is different? Apparently very little. The overall concept of both methods is that production costs are added to the direct costs of products to give the 'full' cost - all costs are dealt with by both methods.

It is the basis and detail of the method of allocation which are different.

## Uses of ABC

Costing products - leading to pricing decisions

Selecting the 'correct' product mix - to maximise product margin or profit

Influencing the design, development and production methods for new processes.

## Activity based costing

If only one product is manufactured, all production costs can be attributed to that product.

In reality the following is likely:

- A range of products is produced;
- The products require the input of common (overhead) resources; and
- The resources are used by the different products in differing proportions.

The amount of overheads is not always directly affected by volume of production.

Terms such as:

- Logistical transactions, balancing transactions, quality transactions and change transactions might be used for grouping overflows.

### Conventional overhead allocation

**Overhead** (may be split by product line)

Divided by volume to give

**Overhead rate**

### Activity based approach

**Overhead**

Collected into cost pools    determined by knowing what causes types of overheads

**Driver based rates**

In essence there is little new in the ABC approach. It can be summarised by defining and using the words 'allocate' and 'absorb' to distinguish between conventional and ABC costing.

Allocation of overheads often means: there is an amount of overhead, the accountant thinks of a way (hopefully sensible) of allocating these to products – from the top down.

Absorption of overheads can mean that the overhead burden has to be absorbed into, or carried by the products. The production manager (reluctantly) accepts a total amount of overhead and, possibly with a more intimate knowledge of the production process, absorbs into a particular product a 'fair' amount of overhead.

Although put forward as a new way of dealing with the question of overhead allocation and thus better full costing of products and services, ABC really is only overhead allocation done in a thoughtful and detailed manner.

The process of activity based costing may be summarised as follows:

- Group overheads in appropriate sets or 'pools'
- List the activities carried on or delivered by these overheads - the pool
- Identify what costs the operation of the activities causes - what the cost 'drivers' are
- Work out overhead rates (overhead recovery rates) for the various activities
- Use these detailed rates to build up the total overhead cost recovery rate for a product component or service unit.

Obviously ABC is potentially very time-consuming and can deliver potentially apparently very accurate costs. At each stage of the process it is important to review which pools, activities, drivers and thus rates are relevant and material to the exercise, the purpose of which must be to deliver adequately detailed overhead cost analysis.

### Establishment of a set of overhead cost pools

The numbers and types of cost pool are decided after identification and assessment of activities which give rise to the need for overhead costs. Not all overheads can have a pool of their own and it is the major causes and drivers of overheads which will predominate in the selection process.

All activities relating to production support should be listed as a starting point in the identification of the cost drivers and definition of cost pools.

## Activities listings

Examples of the possible headings and costs under these are as follows:

Purchasing; Quality Control; Occupancy; Production Scheduling; and Human Resourcing.

## Cost pool analysis

This is a very important stage as the work done here is at the heart of the whole process.The accountant should seek the help of the relevant production manager in identifying overhead costs and what causes or drives them.

When the activities involve labour (as many do), the following questions might be asked.

- Why do we need x people on this activity?
- Why does idle time occur?
- Why is overtime worked on this activity?
- Under what circumstances could we need more?
- Under what circumstances could we need less?
- Could this activity be combined with others?

## Activity based costing – cost pool analysis

Activity Based Costing Cost Pool Analysis

**Purchasing costs**

| Activity | | Resources comsumed Labour costs | Equipment consumables % of labour | Costs | |
|---|---|---|---|---|---|
| A | Requisitioning | 2.00 | 10% | 2.20 | no of requests |
| B | Supplier appraisal | 3.00 | 10% | 3.30 | no of new parts<br>no of orders over 20k |
| C | Purchase order | 2.10 | 10% | 2.31 | no of orders<br>no of suppliers |
| D | Order management | 0.03 | 0% | 0.03 | no of deliveries |
| E | Goods inwards | 1.00 | 10% | 1.10 | no of deliveries<br>size of items |
| F | Approve payment | 0.25 | 10% | 0.28 | no of invoices |
| G | Departmental supervision | 0.05 | 0% | 0.05 | A to D above |

## Matters to be considered when optimising the number of cost drivers

*Relative cost of the overhead pools*

How relevant is the total pool cost compared to other pools – a preliminary review of all potential pools should be carried out to ensure only material ones are further analysed.

How significant are the costs of each pooled activity in relation to the total costs of the pool?

Are all pools of a similar size or are there considerable variations?

*Product diversity*

If there is a high number of product types or variants, this may cause higher levels of overhead.

*Volume diversity*

Where products are produced in different volumes – small batches as opposed to continuous production the small batches may often cause higher overheads.

The above questions could be asked on a preliminary investigation as to whether or not activity based costing may or may not be appropriate. ABC is more likely to be relevant where there are quite distinct types of overhead, in varying amounts, with types and volumes of products which also vary in amount.

## Problems when implementing ABC

**Accuracy of the overhead cost collection system**. How accurate is the costing system? It may be the case that invoice coding, time sheet analysis and accruals calculation are all inadequate to deliver the degree of accuracy required.

**Cost pooling**. Not all pools will be material enough to be separately dealt with and some allocation or re-allocation of costs may be necessary.

**Availability and practicability of cost drivers**. A cost driver must be caused by an activity which is measurable. It should be possible to relate this output. This would not be possible for all costs, for example, general corporate advertising as opposed to specific product marketing and advertising costs.

**Selecting the cost drivers**. It will often be the case that one of several possible cost drivers is appropriate for dealing with pooled costs. It may often appear that a volume based driver is the most obvious to be used. It is particularly important to check whether volume is the prime driver of the pool. This is claimed to be a distinct differentiation between ABC and conventional costing.

**Commonality of costs**. Some overhead costs will be incurred by the general business processes for example machine repair labour costs - which products manufactured on the machine should carry the costs? This indicates that there may be no end to the detailed analysis which can be carried out - a limit to the depth of analysis has to be decided upon and applied consistently.

**Which products should carry the set up costs when switching product lines?** Too much can be made of many such problems and it is the nature of many management accountants to get carried away with finessing to the nth degree. For example, if the whole drive of a business is to offer flexible production with short and ever changing production runs, the set up costs are caused by the general business approach as opposed to one product. If the setting up for a particular product requires higher costs, that product should carry the cost to a greater degree.

### Behavioural aspects

ABC may be resisted on introduction.Therefore as with any new techniques, explanation and training are essential elements of successful introduction and operation of the system.

*There are benefits to be gained from the introduction of ABC:*

- Improved understanding of the costing process – it can be graphically described, rather than be seen as some 'magic' (or maybe dubious!) arbitrary method.
- Increased awareness of what causes costs and thus how product design and production process should be considered.
- Ownership/acceptance of product costs and thus product margins.

### Benefits claimed for ABC

*ABC*

- Is more detailed – it should be more logical and comprehensive
- Provides more accurate product costing
- Improves understanding of cost behaviour
- Provides more meaningful measures – cost driver rates/cost driver volumes.

### Does ABC deliver?

The answer has to be potentially yes, as it is a more thoughtful approach in dealing with overheads.The problem is that benefits may be lost by managers, and particularly accountants, getting tied up in or lost in the welter of detail.

Studies on the success of ABC implementation have indicated that to have a successful outcome, ABC has to be introduced and supported wholeheartedly from the most senior level of management – this is true of most change initiatives. The method, systems and other details have less effect on whether or not ABC will succeed in bringing benefits to a business.

A very simple example of how overheads may be allocated in more detail, using the ABC approach, is set out below:

**Overheads to be allocated**

| | |
|---|---|
| Production | 250,000 |
| Tooling | 90,000 |
| Assembly bay | 540,000 |
| **total overheads** | 880,000 |

**Product details**

| | X | Y | totals |
|---|---|---|---|
| no of units | 20,000 | 5,000 | 25,000 |
| production hours | 8,000 | 5,000 | 13,000 |
| assembly hours | 30,000 | 70,000 | 100,000 |

**Conventional overhead allocation**

| | | | |
|---|---|---|---|
| **on basis of no of units** | 880,000 / 25,000 | = | **35.20 per unit for X and Y** |
| proof 35.20 x | 25,000 | = | **880,000** |
| **on basis of assembly labour** | 880,000 / 100,000 | = | **8.80 per assembly hour** |

| Overhead per unit | | **X** | **Y** |
|---|---|---|---|
| hours in assembly per unit | hours / units | 30,000 / 20,000 | 70,000 / 5,000 |
| | = | 1.50 | 14.00 |
| **on basis of assembly labour** | | **13.20** | **123.20** |

| | | | |
|---|---|---|---|
| proof 20000 x | 13.20 | = | 264,000 |
| 5000 x | 123.20 | = | 616,000 |
| | | | **880,000** |

## Activity based cost overhead allocation

**Overhead activity analysis** — **unit per component**

| **Cost pool** | **Driver** | **X** | **Y** | **totals** |
|---|---|---|---|---|
| Production | machine hours | 8,000 | 5,000 | 13,000 |
| Tooling | set up time – hours | 1,000 | 4,000 | 5,000 |
| Assembly bay | labour hours | 30,000 | 70,000 | 100,000 |

| | | | | | | | **per unit** | |
|---|---|---|---|---|---|---|---|---|
| | | | | | | | **X** | **Y** |
| Production | 250,000 / 13,000 | = | 19.23 per m/c hr | **X** 8,000 / 20,000 | = | 0.40 | 7.69 | |
| | | | | **Y** 5,000 / 5,000 | = | 1.00 | | 19.23 |
| Tooling | 90,000 / 5,000 | = | 18.00 per hr | **X** 1,000 / 20,000 | = | 0.05 | 0.90 | |
| | | | | **Y** 4,000 / 5,000 | | 0.80 | | 14.40 |
| Assembly | 540,000 / 100,000 | = | 5.40 per hr | **X** 30,000 / 20,000 | = | 1.50 | 8.10 | |
| | | | | **Y** 70,000 / 5,000 | = | 14.00 | | 75.60 |
| **on detailed or ABC basis** | | | | | | | **16.69** | **109.23** |

| proof | | | | | | |
|---|---|---|---|---|---|---|
| | 20,000 units | x | at | 16.69 | = | 333,846 |
| | 5,000 units | x | at | 109.23 | = | 546,154 |
| | | | | | | 880,000 |

## Checklist

- ✓ What are your problems with overheads?
- ✓ Identify the level of detailed analysis required.
- ✓ Activity based costing may help.

# Budgeting

## Introduction – the operating budget

## Why budget?

## Budget stages explained

## How to budget

## Checklist

## Introduction – the operating budget

The word 'budgeting' may be used in many contexts. For example, there is budgeting of sales or output, costs, profit, resources, cash and capital expenditure. The reasons for budgeting, forecasting or anticipating figures are many, the most obvious being as a means of measuring performance and thus controlling a business. This chapter deals with budgeting sales, costs and thus profit (or loss!) – the budgeted profit and loss account anticipated for the future, or what could be termed the 'operating budget'. Budgeting of cash and capital expenditure are dealt with in Chapter 7. The reasons for budgeting profit and loss focus on the key issue of taking the business forward and delivering results.

The term used in this chapter is operating budget, as it is presumed that for most readers the purpose of budgets has to do with the running of a business of whatever kind, and it is the expected figures for sales, costs and resultant profit or loss in which people are interested.

## Why budget?

Before anyone budgets or asks others to budget it is most important that the reasons for and objectives of the budgeting exercise are known and set down in writing.

Reasons often given for budgeting:

- To control
- To plan resources
- To plan cash
- To achieve a goal
- To manage the business
- To achieve the business' objectives
- To fulfil the business's strategic plan.

All of the above are valid reasons for budgeting and those which individuals consider to be most important will relate to their perceived purpose of budgeting and the level within the organisation at which the budget is to be used. An operating budget is compiled for and used for many purposes, but unless its prime use is based on clear (stated) objectives the budgeting exercise will not deliver results and may well be a very hollow exercise.

## Budget stages explained

### The stages of the budget process

*Each stage of the budget process is defined below:*

*A Set/know objectives*

Overall objectives will come from the corporate plan or equivalent. There must be much consideration of budget objectives and the strategy and tactics required to achieve them during the detailed work required in assembling and determining the corporate plan – see B 'Arrange strategy' below.

Objectives should be set down in writing in an ordered manner – principal objective first, followed by sub objectives, with constraints and conflicts clearly noted. Examples of setting out budget objectives are on pages 304 to 306.

*B Arrange strategy and tactics*

The word 'strategy' is used here in the mundane sense of considering the actions to be taken, the order in which they are undertaken and the facilities required to achieve the budget objectives. The arranging of day to day strategy and tactics required to deliver the strategy must be considered during preparation of the detailed corporate plan and regularly reviewed.

*C Prepare detailed plan – the budget*

This is the stage where the budget is prepared – the pieces of paper with figures on them which are used to monitor the business's activities over the following periods.

Budget figures will only be of real value where there are clear budget objectives – goals to be achieved.

There is no particular skill required in budgeting - just a knowledge of the income or costs which may be made or incurred whilst meeting the business's objectives. See How to budget below.

*D Implement the budget*

If the budget prepared under C is of any use, it ought to be implemented. Implementation will mean different things to different organisations, eg the sending of a brief memo or holding a formal budget implementation meeting, through to entering into a budget 'contract' with staff.

*E Monitor the budget and actual figures – take action*

Budgets exist to help the business achieve its objectives, but they also exist for control purposes - this is very much the case with the detailed manufacturing or operational budgets. The budget figures are benchmarks - what is expected when operating in the expected conditions - therefore any deviation from budget indicates that there may be problems and thus action should be taken to bring the business back into the desired operational position.

*F Feedback/review objectives*

A business should not change its course or overall objectives just because the budget is not being achieved. However, if there is consistent deviation from the budget, there is reason to question the budget and the underlying objectives of the business function in operation.

## How to budget

If you have responsibility for the entire budget process, the above stages should be followed in a logical order. However, it is more often the case that the manager is asked to budget after the objectives and strategy/tactics have been set. Hopefully the setting of detailed objectives will have been done in consultation with the managers and staff who have to budget and thus deliver results. Whether starting with defined objectives or being given them, 'how to budget' becomes a matter of finding the figures to put on the budget forms. The paragraphs and illustration below demonstrate methods of doing this.

## Know objectives

To be able to budget, the objectives of the business ought to be known and expressed in a clear quantified manner, for example, sales to grow by at least 10% year on year; margins to be maintained at 15%; costs to be minimised, that is, at last year's levels or lower.

It is possible to budget without knowledge of the company's overall objectives, more so down the line where budgets tend to be used for detailed control purposes. However, at middle and senior levels in the company budgeting will not really deliver results if the budget figures are not linked to the company's objectives.

## Forecast figures

The word forecasting is defined and used in many ways in business. Common usage with respect to the budget process is simply the 'expert' estimating future sales or costs. For some situations, the 'expert' – the experienced manager – having clear unambiguous objectives, and knowledge of the current business environment, can produce accurate and reliable forecasts. There are also many mathematical techniques and others which rely on sophisticated data collection and interpretation. The detailed methods will tend to be specific to the industry and beyond the scope of this book. An example is forecasting sales for a supermarket chain; data will be held for every day of past years and weeks and figures can be forecast from these as a base, taking account of weather, holidays etc.

## Using existing data

Past experience or experience from a similar business is a practical starting point. Even when taking this simple approach to budgeting, the point that each new period is 'new' should not be forgotten and updating previous figures by simple factors arising from sales volume increases or because of inflation is not good enough.

## Completing the budget

Traditional management accounting texts talk of the 'master budget' which comprised sales budgets, production budgets, direct costs budgets, overhead budgets and so on. This breakdown may well still be appropriate for some businesses and a suitable structure for budget compilation is important.

At this stage we shall assume that the structure is in place, the question being how to put figures into the budget. There are really only two methods as discussed above:

- Use existing data on income and costs, updating with relevant known factors; and
- Forecasting and researching to come up with appropriate new figures.

Updating existing data is obvious enough and for many situations may be the only acceptable method.

What is meant by researching? As an example, this may be formal, detailed market research to yield expected sales figures or more likely something as mundane as recording, for a trial period, the use of the photocopier to establish a reasonable figure for photocopying costs. There is no magic source of budget figures, some work has to be done.

The word new in italics above makes the point that what is required for good budgeting is the obtaining of figures which relate to the current objectives, budgeting for today's activities – simply updating previous figures is really not good enough.

**Illustration**

You have taken over as manager of an established branch office of a financial services company and have to produce the operating budget for next year.

In spite of market conditions being tough, new business sales are expected to grow by 6% minimum with the company-wide launch of new products.

Head office has indicated that overall costs should be at a similar level to last year. This is at a time when general inflation is approximately 3%.

**Restate objectives** for yourself and staff.

**Review** last year's figures - budget and actual. Why do cost headings exist? Challenge the level of sales and costs.

Discuss with staff how sales, particularly the new products, can be increased by local effort, and quantify any costs of local promotion and advertising. Is it possible that sales could be increased by more than 6%?

Discuss how costs can be reduced. Obviously, focus on the larger figures first.

**Prepare a draft** budget - does this meet or exceed head office criteria?

**Decide** on necessary action to meet criteria - with possible further discussion with staff.

**Implement** the budget - have on record the final budget and the assumptions underlying the figures. Let staff know how the budget criteria will be met and the effort required from all.

The above illustration could be adapted to suit most budgeting situations.

## Examples of different styles/culture when putting budget objectives on record

### A XYZ plc

*MEMO*

From ____________________

To ____________________

____________________

Date ____________________

*Subject*

**Customer Service Department Budget Preparation year to 31 December ____**

### Budget objectives

| | |
|---|---|
| **Principal:** | **to achieve a return on investment of 14% minimum** |
| Subsidiary: | to increase sales (higher margin servicing) by 12% |
| | to maintain operating costs at today's level – an effective decrease in operating costs per service hour of 11% |
| Constraint: | average response time to be maintained at no more than 120 mins – at present the average response time is 112 mins. |

This minimum return is 2% higher than that achieved to date but can be achieved by increasing sales of higher margin work and controlling costs as explained and discussed at the department meeting of _________.

**Commentary:** **overall objectives and thus goals are clear**

**constraints are considered**

**more detail is required.**

## B Budget contract

between **executive board budget committee** and **Mr A B – controller**, process division.

The company's key measures of success this year are a return on capital employed of 14% minimum and free cash flow in excess of each divisions declared accounting profit.

In respect of the process division this can be achieved by:

A keeping refurbishment and major overhaul spend at a level no greater than current historical cost depreciation.

B reducing operating costs by 3% overall.

C maintaining plant availability at 94% or better.

Charge out costs for processing will be constant and remain the responsibility of product division.

### *The contract*

You have accepted that these targets, whilst tight, are achievable and your division has the task of meeting these objectives.

The budgets for A capital expenditure should be prioritised and have maximum necessary spend no greater than $970,000

The budgets for B operating costs allow a total spend of $1,940,000

Availability will be monitored by product division and their budgets are based on plant availability of 94%.

**Commentary:** **Overall objectives and thus goals are clear**

**Very formal – what happens if the 'contract' is not met?**

**Does the process division controller have sub-contracts with his staff?**

### C Budget memo

***to General Managers • Luxe Hotel Division***

It is time to consider drawing up the budget objectives, and the strategy and tactics for achieving these next year.

The outlook for this trade sector is one of sales growth with improved margins, although competition remains fierce.

Overall the company must consider making an adequate return on assets, although at this stage no precise targets will be given.

Also due to dividend payment pressures the divisions must generate adequate free cash flow.

These objectives can be met by tightly controlling capital spend, increasing occupancy and improving margins.

To enable headquarters to set the divisions budget objectives General Managers are requested to suggest ways in which the above general objectives may be achieved for their respective establishments.

**Commentary:** **Consultative in approach – a preliminary stage**

**Overall objectives and thus goals are clear but unquantified**

**Properly collated and analysed, the comments on how to achieve the objectives could yield very useful, practical budget directives**

**Capital spend is restricted, but not maintenance is this the intention?**

**Presumably GMs and staff understand exactly what terms like 'free cash flow' mean.**

### Sales Targets and Selling costs – year to 31 December 2xx7

***to Manager • North Central Region***

*Sales target for your area is:*

890,000 (850,000 last year)    achieved last year 860,000

Monthly targets are 45,000 in January and December and 80,000 all other months.

*Discount budget*

You can give up to 5% discount as inducement – the total budget for this cost is 30,000 for the year.

*Travel/subsistence costs*

Total allowance for the year is 8,400 and total mileage max 33,000.

Expenditure in excess of 700 per month must be explained, as must mileage above 2,500 miles per month.

**Commentary:** **Overall objectives and thus goals are specific**

**What happens if targets are exceeded? Is there reward?**

**Is manager meant to manage the detailed spend?**

## Checklist

- ✓ Set/know objectives.
- ✓ Research and think.
- ✓ Discuss.
- ✓ Draft.
- ✓ Decide/discuss.
- ✓ Do.

*section two*

# Budgeting

**Setting budget objectives**

**Where do budget objectives come from?**

**Budget objectives and company culture**

**Budgeting systems and techniques**

**Checklist**

**Budgeting can:**

- **Take the business forward (new strategies and direction)**
- **Provide direction**
- **Assist in resource allocation and management**
- **Provide a basis for control**
- **Motivate (or de-motivate) people**

**What does budgeting do for you? What does your company expect budgeting to do?**

**This section explores the budget process in more detail, in particular considering: determination of budget objectives, the need for company culture and budgeting method to be in harmony, and the use of Zero Based Budgeting (ZBB) techniques to develop thoughtful, more focused and more accurate budgets.**

## Setting budget objectives

An operational budget sets down in figures the intended outcome of a business's activities for a period.

There are several reasons for doing this but the principal ones are:

- To set clear objectives for the business
- To consider the resources required to meet the business's objectives
- To monitor or control the business.

To be able to budget, the objectives of the business must be known and wherever possible expressed in a quantified manner. A logical order of (quantified) budget objectives is as follows:

- **To make a return on capital employed or invested > 20%**
- **To achieve a net margin of at least 7%**
- **To achieve sales of 1m.**

Most often a manager deals with one or more sub-objectives, for example, budgeting for increased volume of business - sales.

There will be budget objectives which may conflict with the principal objectives, eg excellent response times to customers' requirements may cause over manning, higher labour costs and lower net profit.

There will also be constraints, eg meeting statutory requirements on health and safety - these cannot be ignored.

Obviously the principal objective of a business or department must be clearly stated and known to those preparing the detailed budgets. Also, it may be relevant to consider and make clear to all involved in the budget process whether or not the overall and sub-objectives are long or short-term, eg customer response times could be cut to meet budget cost control requirements this year, but this may not affect (cause a decline in) sales until next year.

## Where do budget objectives come from?

It is the author's view that these should clearly come from the chief executive and board. There are instances where, due to a lack of ability by the executives, company staff have been requested or driven to come up with the objectives of their business. Certainly it is a great waste not to draw on the combined ability of the staff in identifying opportunities and developing business objectives, strategies and tactics, but ultimately the chief executive and the board should set the objectives.

It might be said that a board who leave the staff to come up with the objectives have abrogated their duties.

The use of the word 'driven' above indicates another aspect of the budget process. How does the company operate from a relationship point of view?

Extremes might be:

**A** The board - really a single powerful chief executive determines the company objectives, overall and in great detail, and commands that managers run their areas with these budget figures - a dictatorial approach. This may well work for some businesses, the problems being, whether staff like working in such an environment. Presumably yes, or else they leave. Also there are many people who are happy to work with predetermined budgets - they just have to get on with the job!

The serious weakness with the dictatorial approach is that there is the need for a continuing succession of wise, all-knowing chief executives. One misdirecting or poor chief executive and the business falters or fails.

**B** The board, led by the chief executive sets (sometimes vague) overall objectives, leaving managers free to interpret and action them. This again may well work for some businesses. Competent managers of similar standing know what has to be delivered and arrange their activities to achieve their sub objectives which will achieve the business's overall objectives. The problems with this approach are that different managers may interpret the company's overall objectives in different ways and, more seriously, whilst managers may be of similar standing, one or more managers may have the ability to ensure that their particular objectives are achieved in priority to any others - the business revolves around them.

The above illustrations highlight the need for the budget process to be thought out from the top - where responsibility lies! The budget process has to be managed and lead! The budget process and personnel involved have to work in harmony.

It is quite common within an organisation that different approaches are possible and in fact desirable. For example, there could be an excellent sales team, which functions well and delivers. Their views are sought on budgeted levels of sales, but in fact the actual budgets (more in the form of targets) are set (dictatorially) by the sales director. The sales team may complain (a little!) but in fact are happy to have the given budget (target) figures to achieve.

## Budget objectives and company culture

The overall objective of the company should be to deliver an adequate return on capital employed or invested. This is a well established objective in many of the world's most successful companies. To deliver the adequate return specified the company has to be driven or lead forward. The question as to 'who drives the company' is important generally and specifically when it comes to ensuring that the budget process delivers.

Who drives the company? The answer must be the board through the chief executive. But what this question means to elicit is what particular function. By function is meant, for example, production, finance, sales and marketing, human resource, personnel or procurement for example.

Common wisdom today is that companies are 'customer driven' - this may be correct, but those involved in setting up the budget process really have to ask which function in their organisation drives the business or is the lead function. The board and chief executive should ensure harmony amongst the functions and thus in the budget process, but there are very many instances where this does not happen. You then get say, sales and marketing carrying out very good market research and producing realistic sales budgets, but the actual detailed sales, cost and profit budgets (based on company objectives) being assembled by the finance function - planning and budgeting are carried out as separate exercises.

The point being made is that the company must have clearly stated objectives **and** the budget process should be lead by the function which ultimately drives the business.

Who drives your business? Most likely the customer, but this need not always be the case.

One reason that another function may be the driving force is human weakness - the head of the function, whilst not the most senior board or even staff member, is however, by personality, the one around whom the business revolves. For example, a very dominant engineering/production director, whilst aware of the company's overall requirement to make an adequate return and to increase margins, may have a fixed idea that the production process runs non-stop, with long production runs of each product - it is then up to sales to sell the products!

It is important to identify which function drives a business (this may change over time).The customer and therefore sales may be the most important. However,for say the hotel industry, whilst sales, and particularly human resource functions are very important, it might be argued that the industry is a mature one and it is control of margins and costs which is paramount - the finance function may be the driving force.

## Budgeting systems and techniques

### Challenging the budget figures – ZZB (zero based budgeting)

Before studying the particular technique of zero based budgeting – ZBB – it is important to consider whether or not particular accounting systems, reporting methods and reports can lead to better budgeting.

The answer must be yes. However, it is a common mistake to believe that just by purchasing a new system – spending more on IT – all will be well.

### The need for commitment

Companies which successfully budget, whether at the top level with the corporate plan or at the detailed level of controlling day to day costs, have one thing in common – they are committed to the budget process. However the budgets are prepared and collated and however and whatever reports are produced, the entire staff are aware of their meaning and are expected to respond to the figures.

**The budget process is meant to achieve objectives (and also assist control).**

### Reporting structure

The reporting structure should fit the needs of and the culture of the business.

### Report layout

Reports should have the (minimum) necessary detail to give the required information and facilitate response or action.

## Zero based budgeting

As indicated in the previous session on budgeting, those companies and individuals who are successful at budgeting are those who have a clear purpose for budgeting - clear objectives - and then follow a distinct, consistent path during the budget process.

The principal concepts within zero based budgeting - ZBB - are not new; they are to be found in many organisations' budgeting processes. It should be noted that while many companies adopt a zero based approach in their annual budgeting exercise this may not be a true in depth ZBB process, but rather a use of the general principles.

However, it is sensible to study ZBB and its underlying concepts as they illustrate how budgeting may be improved and the whole budgeting process made to deliver results.

### *ZBB considers*

**What means are available for achieving a certain result**

**What (possibly) varying effort levels exist in achieving the required result**

At its heart ZBB questions:

- **Why is a cost incurred?**
- **Is incurring the cost necessary?**
- **What level(s) of effort are required?**
- **How can resources best be used?**

**At all times these questions are asked with knowledge of the organisation's overall, divisional, departmental, profit or cost centre objectives.**

For many businesses it is also possible to consider the priorities when incurring costs and the description Priority Based Costing might be used.

The concept of ZBB would appear to have come from the United States in the 1950s and it appears to have been devised or at least recommended for Government spending agencies, State Authorities, etc. There are several published commentaries on the adoption and implementation of the system in the 1960s, some attempts successful, others not.

Implementation failures are a useful reminder that the whole process of ZBB requires proper implementation - understanding of its true nature by those involved, adequate time for implementation and commitment and constant review of the implementation process. This, of course, is also true for any budgeting exercise and indicates that much of what can be delivered by a proper ZBB exercise could also be delivered by a proper commitment to the existing budgeting process.

## Weaknesses of traditional budgeting and how ZBB differs

Traditional budgeting may also be termed incremental budgeting, where the word 'incremental' is considered to relate to the small (in relation to the total costs) changes in cost which occur in any business, year on year, as activities change. These changes are normally incremental increases, and thus traditional cost budgets often 'creep' up in amount.

The defects of the traditional approach are that whilst it is simple to comprehend, it often misses what budgeting should really be about - achieving today's business objectives - not just updating previous figures incrementally or marginally - at its simplest and worst - adding 5% to costs because of general inflation!

Objectives or policy options considered are only those incrementally different from the base position. Therefore the marginal values of objectives and constraints and a relatively small amount of the total cost may be subject to review, rather than the total costs being budgeted.

ZBB is a planning as well as a budgeting tool; it is the systematic expression of the business's overall and detailed objectives in quantified form. It considers the need for, the amount, and the priority of a spend. Only when functions, activities or projects are selected which achieve the objectives of a business might it be said that the business's budgeting system is delivering.

ZBB is meant to involve all levels of management, although some aspects of the approach could be and often are in operation in a 'top down', 'dictatorial' management structure.

A common method of implementation is to have **the board** of a company:

- Establish overall objectives for the company
- Establish detailed objectives for each division, profit centre etc (in consultation with managers)
- Set outline amounts for expenditure for the period under review.

With these overall budget parameters **operating managers** are in a position to:

- Define their detailed objectives
- Propose methods of achieving their objectives
- Cost the necessary resources
- Prioritise objectives/methods where possible.

**The costed and prioritised tasks are reviewed**

**Priorities are reviewed from the overall company objectives rather than just from the local, detailed objectives.**

**The available resources may then be allocated.**

This may not appear too different from what many companies do under conventional budgeting and indeed it could be argued that ZBB is just good budgeting. However there remains the distinction that ZBB starts from a zero base – a clean sheet of paper – and questions the costs and resources required to achieve all the principal and detailed objectives in a logical and prioritised manner.

These notes continue further to give an outline of how detailed ZBB may become.

As mentioned at the outset what many companies call zero based budgeting is really only using the concept of questioning afresh each year the need for and amount of an expense – starting from a zero base. Detailed ZBB is more than this.

The stages are as follows:

- **Split each company activity into discrete decision packages (DPs)**
- **Quantify (cost or possibly revenue) and rank all decision packages**
- **Logically allocate resources.**

There follows an example of a decision package for one activity. A perusal of this identifies the following positive aspects of a ZBB exercise:

a **Activities** have to be identified and **defined** – cost centres or areas should not just be able to exist unquestioned. The activity is given a name or reference and described.

b Someone has to take, using the popular word, **ownership** of the activity and its related costs or income.

c Budgets must be formally reviewed.

d Budgets have to be based on company objectives.

e Activities have to be defined.

f Alternative approaches are invited – be positive – how might objectives be achieved?

g Cost/revenues, suitably analysed have to be given - the sources of the data should be stated.

h Performance measures, how achievement may be measured should be identified at the outset.

i To assist in identifying whether a cost/revenue is essential the effect of not budgeting for it should be quantified. This also should assist with ranking activities.

j The benefits of approval should be quantified - also there is scope for detailing relevant less tangible benefits, again this may assist with ranking the activities.

k Costs (or revenues) have to be ranked in order of importance, or prioritised.

## Problems in implementing a ZBB system

a Can all a company's activities be identified - is it necessary to analyse them all?

b Does the company really give ownership to individuals?

k Is it possible to set up a **fair** system of ranking all the various activities which are to be found throughout a company?

Whilst there may not be many problems, those that do exist really centre on the fact that for many situations the whole exercise may involve much unnecessary and in the end unproductive analysis.

**However, the use of an analysis sheet below could help anyone who has to focus on what their budget is for and how it may be defined and quantified to meet their company objectives.**

g

## XYZ Inc

***ZBB Decision Analysis Package*** Date ________

Activity a ________________________________

Ranking k ________________________________

Responsible personnel b ________________________

Reviewer c ________________________________

| Objectives d |
| --- |
| Outline description e |
| Alternatives f |
| Projected costs/revenues g |
| Performance measures h |
| Effect of non approval i |
| Benefits of approving j |

### ZBB and company structure and culture

ZBB will be more appropriate for some companies and activities than for others.

Firstly, the nature of some businesses is significant. For example, those producing many products or providing services in different divisions may get more from detailed ZBB analysis than a business supplying principally a single service. However, as stated at the outset the principles underlying the ZBB approach really have much to commend them as they are at the heart of any good budgeting process.

Secondly, the management structure and for that matter, the culture of an organisation may be ill-suited to the ZBB approach, for example where the culture does not require or encourage people to take ownership of their budgets - budgets are really crude control (or incentive!) tools.

### Summary

The principles of the ZBB approach are not new and there is often no need to carry out a detailed ZBB exercise, but many budgeting exercises could be improved by adopting some of the ZBB techniques where appropriate.

## Checklist

- ✓ Budgeting must be objective based.
- ✓ The budget process must be lead.
- ✓ The budget process should be in harmony.
- ✓ ZBB techniques may help.

# Other titles from Thorogood

### 501 Questions and Answers for Company Directors and Company Secretaries

*Roger Mason*

£18.99 paperback, ISBN 1 85418 340 0
Published June 2005

An exhaustive reference covering literally everything the Company Director and Company Secretary needs to know: clearly arranged by subject matter, easy to use and providing speedy access to guidance, facts and figures, law and best practice, this is an expert book written in a no-nonsense, jargon free style.

### The A-Z of Management Concepts and Models

*B. Karlof and F. Lovingsson*

£18.99 paperback, ISBN 1 85418 390 7 • £35.00 hardback, ISBN 1 85418 385 0
Published May 2005

An A to Z of all the essential concepts and models applied in business and management, from Balanced scorecard and the Boston matrix to Experience curve, Kaizen, McKinsey's 7S model, Market analysis, Porter's generic strategies, Relative cost position, Sustainable development to Yield management and Zero-based planning.

### The A-Z of Employment Practice

*David Martin*

£19.99 paperback, ISBN 1 85418 380 X • £42.00 hardback, ISBN 1 85418 300 1
Published November 2004

This book provides comprehensive, practical guidance on personnel law and practice at a time when employers are faced with a maze of legislation, obligations and potential penalties. It provides detailed and practical advice on what to do and how to do it.

The A to Z format ensures that sections appear under individual headings for instant ease of reference. The emphasis is not so much on the law as on its implications; the advice is expert, clear and practical, with a minimum of legal references. Checklists, procedures and examples are all given as well as warnings on specific pitfalls.

### Gurus on Business Strategy

*Tony Grundy*

£14.99 paperback, ISBN 1 85418 262 5 • £24.99 hardback, ISBN 1 85418 222 6
Published June 2003

This book is a one-stop guide to the world's most important writers on business strategy. It expertly summarises all the key strategic concepts and describes the work and contribution of each of the leading thinkers in the field.

It goes further: it analyses the pro's and con's of many of the key theories in practice and offers two enlightening case-studies. The third section of the book provides a series of detailed checklists to aid you in the development of your own strategies for different aspects of the business.

More than just a summary of the key concepts, this book offers valuable insights into their application in practice.

### Gurus on e-business

*John Middleton*

£14.99 paperback, ISBN 1 85418 386 9 • £24.99 hardback, ISBN 1 85418 381 8
Published February 2006

This book explores the impact and significance of e-business as illustrated by the work and thinking of a number of key players in the field. This accessible guide is for business people looking to make optimal and profitable use of e-business. Includes gurus from Tim Berners-Lee and Michael Dell to Bill Gates and Shoshana Zuboff.

### The Complete Guide to International Financial Reporting Standards

Including IAS and interpretation

*Ralph Tiffin*

£18.99 paperback, ISBN 1 85418 279 X • £35.00 hardback, ISBN 1 85418 274 9
Published April 2004

This book is not a re-write of the standards but rather summarises the issues which give rise to the standard practice, explaining the accounting and disclosure requirements and practical problems of compliance. The accounting ideas behind them and the effect on financial statements of each of the Standards, is explained.

personal and professional development has been proven to provide an outstanding ROI through increased productivity in both you and your team. Ultimately leading to a dramatic impact on the bottom line.

With this in mind Falconbury have developed a comprehensive portfolio of training programmes to enable managers of all levels to develop their skills in leadership, communications, finance, people management, change management and all areas vital to achieving success in today's commercial environment.

### What Falconbury can offer you?

- Practical applied methodology with a proven results
- Extensive bank of experienced trainers
- Limited attendees to ensure one-to-one guidance
- Up to the minute thinking on management and leadership techniques
- Interactive training
- Balanced mix of theoretical and practical learning
- Learner-centred training
- Excellent cost/quality ratio

### Falconbury In-Company Training

Falconbury are aware that a public programme may not be the solution to leadership and management issues arising in your firm. Involving only attendees from your organisation and tailoring the programme to focus on the current challenges you face individually and as a business may be more appropriate. With this in mind we have brought together our most motivated and forward thinking trainers to deliver tailored in-company programmes developed specifically around the needs within your organisation.

All our trainers have a practical commercial background and highly refined people skills. During the course of the programme they act as facilitator, trainer and mentor, adapting their style to ensure that each individual benefits equally from their knowledge to develop new skills.

Falconbury works with each organisation to develop a programme of training that fits your needs.

### Mentoring and coaching

Developing and achieving your personal objectives in the workplace is becoming increasingly difficult in today's constantly changing environment. Additionally, as a manager or leader, you are responsible for guiding colleagues towards the realisation of their goals. Sometimes it is easy to lose focus on your short and long-term aims.

Falconbury's one-to-one coaching draws out individual potential by raising self-awareness and understanding, facilitating the learning and performance development that creates excellent managers and leaders. It builds renewed self-confidence and a strong sense of 'can-do' competence, contributing significant benefit to the organisation. Enabling you to focus your energy on developing your potential and that of your colleagues.

Mentoring involves formulating winning strategies, setting goals, monitoring achievements and motivating the whole team whilst achieving a much improved work life balance.

falconbury
BUSINESS LAW SEMINARS